Washington's Haunted Hotspots

Linda Moffitt

Schiffer Publishing Ltd®

4880 Lower Valley Road, Atglen, Pennsylvania 19310

Schiffer Books are available at special discounts for bulk purchases for sales promotions or premiums. Special editions, including personalized covers, corporate imprints, and excerpts can be created in large quantities for special needs. For more information contact the publisher:

Schiffer Publishing Ltd.
4880 Lower Valley Road
Atglen, PA 19310
Phone: (610) 593-1777; Fax: (610) 593-2002
E-mail: Info@schifferbooks.com

For the largest selection of fine reference books on this and related subjects, please visit our web site at **www.schifferbooks.com.**
We are always looking for people to write books on new and related subjects. If you have an idea for a book please contact us at the above address.

This book may be purchased from the publisher. Include $5.00 for shipping. Please try your bookstore first. You may write for a free catalog.

In Europe, Schiffer books are distributed by
Bushwood Books
6 Marksbury Ave.
Kew Gardens
Surrey TW9 4JF England
Phone: 44 (0) 20 8392-8585; Fax: 44 (0) 20 8392-9876
E-mail: info@bushwoodbooks.co.uk
Website: www.bushwoodbooks.co.uk

Designed by Stephanie Daugherty
Type set in Demon Night/New Baskerville BT
ISBN: 978-0-7643-3277-7
Printed in The United States of America

DEDICATION

This book is dedicated to my husband for his support and encouragement as well as his endless patience driving me to haunted locales; and for giving me my inspiration, my son, Matthew.

ACKNOWLEDGMENTS

I wish to sincerely thank my parents for helping me put this book together and my father for his photographic talent. Not to forget the dozens of people all over Washington State and beyond who told me their stories to make this book happen.

Word of Caution

Many of the hotspots in this book are military bases, hospitals, private residences, state institutions, and businesses. Please be respectful when visiting any of the locals listed. Obey all signs and pay all the appropriate fees. If the locale is a private residence, please stay an appropriate distance and always get permission first before approaching the property. Many of the sites are patrolled by authorities and trespassers will be prosecuted.

I also want to note that some of the owners are not open to the idea there may be a ghost or spirit present, nor are they welcoming of people looking for ghosts or asking questions about ghosts; please respect their wishes.

I cannot stress enough to be respectful and obey all laws and signs when visiting these sites.

I have tried my best to authenticate all the stories in this book; many of the stories are a combination of stories that I have gathered from multiple interviews. I have also tried to give the most current information available.

CONTENTS

Introduction

    I have been reading, visiting, and researching haunted locations for as long as I can remember. If and why ghosts are real is secondary to my desire to see or relive history. It is one thing to see a statue, costume, or relic in a museum; it is quite another to see the past come to life—to hear the old music, people talking and laughing, pool balls clinking, or even to smell the perfume or cigar smoke of times gone by, and of course, I love getting the willies and the excitement of visiting a haunted location.

    The stories of people who once lived are romantic, tragic, and sometimes unusual or unknown. I provide as much information to guide you to these locations as possible. Included are directions and I have tried to produce an easy route from one site to the next. As with anything, please use common sense and take into account that roads may change, businesses move or close, buildings are torn down, and access is opened or closed off. As always, please check before visiting; be respectful of the spirits as well as the building and other visitors or guests. Some locations may need reservations or permissions granted first. Never trespass on private property.

TIPS FOR SLEEPING WITH THE HAUNTS

If you are planning to stay at one of the haunted accommodations, here are a few words of advice. Make sure you choose a haunting suitable for you. If you want to be terrified all night long, choose a haunting which will scare you; if you want to try and get some sleep, choose less of a scare-factor haunting or perhaps sleep in a room that isn't necessarily haunted. If you want to stay in a haunted room on Halloween night go ahead, but the ghosts don't care that it's Halloween, only the proprietors do and you will surely pay more, and more than likely, not have a ghostly experience due to the extra noise from the festivities.

Make sure you do your research and speak with the hotel employees about history and the ghosts. Have there have been any recent experiences? What are the hotspots? You never know how you are going to react if something does happen. Have an escape plan; check out alternative hotels in the area, just in case you need to leave in the middle of the night. Lastly, leave your children at home, they may be as enthusiastic about being scared or seeing a spirit as you are, but they do not know how to handle this and it may cause problems in the future.

GHOSTLY SUPERSTITIONS AND PROTECTIONS

More than 3,000 years ago, in Athens Greece, the first documented ghost sighting may have occurred to a man named Athendorus who rented a house that was rumored to be haunted. One night, he heard a rattling noise and saw a man in chains. Suddenly, the spirit pointed to the ground, then disappeared. The next day, workers dug up a skeleton in the garden of the home. Athendorus had the body properly buried in the cemetery and the ghost was never seen again.

Ghosts of ancient times usually had something to say, unlike today where they just seem to hang around scaring the living or finding that they are trapped somehow. Many people throughout the years are very superstitious and ghosts are no exception; one account of this is about lilies, which may explain why they are a favorite flower to put in the hands of a deceased before burial. Other superstitions tell of lilies spontaneously appearing on the graves of people executed for crimes they did not commit. Some believe that planting lilies in a garden will protect the area from ghosts and evil spirits.

During my research, I have uncovered many odd superstitions regarding ghosts. One legend wants you to turn your pockets out if you pass a cemetery, or where someone has died recently, to insure you will not take a ghost home in your pocket. Another strange tale warns that if you see a ghost, you should walk around it nine times, and if you cannot

do this, crow like a rooster to fool the ghost into thinking dawn is coming and that it should leave promptly.

No matter if you are superstitious or not, you may want to take some more sensible protection with you to ensure a spirit does not follow you home during your adventures. Through history salt has always provided protection. Legends states that ghosts can't cross it and generally do not like the substance. Sprinkle salt across your entrances, and hang it in a vile in front of your windows, or for personal protection, wear it around your neck. Lodestone, if worn, will help you avoid an encounter with an evil spirit. Finally, put houseleeks on your roof; ghosts cannot bear to be close to this plant. Its name means *ever living* in Latin. Houseleeks are a succulent plant; the most common variety is the Hen-and-chickens. You can find most houseleeks at your local nursery.

Talking to Ghosts

In 1848, a movement called spiritualism started in Hydesville, New York. The Fox sisters claimed to communicate with the dead through rapping sounds. Even though the sisters eventually admitted to making it up, the movement they started stuck and continues today, including whole towns that are devoted to speaking with the dead.

Intelligent Hauntings

There are several different types of ghosts or hauntings. Intelligent hauntings are spirits who can interact with the living. They whisper, slam doors, create cold spots or temperature drops, they will touch you or tug on your clothing or hair; reports of being slapped have even arisen. They can create smells, such as cigar smoke, for instance. Often, they move items around or hide them only to make them reappear later, and sometimes they even break things. These ghosts could be nice, helpful, or mean; they usually have the same personality as they did in life. Intelligent hauntings contain the energy of the person who has died. That is why people often sense intense feelings. Anger or sadness, for example, may create a heavy feeling in a room or place, or even a feeling of dread will come over you.

Residual Hauntings

Residual hauntings are memories or recordings of an event that continues to replay itself over time, for example, a woman staring out a window waiting for her husband, or even a train heading down a track which may or may not still be there. If a ghost walks through a wall, that's probably because, at the time, there was a door at the location. The ghost does not know that a new wall has been put up. If only half the ghost appears, that's because the floor or ground level has changed since the ghost was alive. The appearance and action are always the same and the ghost is always unaware of the living.

POLTERGEIST

A poltergeist is the movement of objects—aggressive eruptions of activity. Some researchers believe that young girls can cause this phenomenon, which is an unknowing use of certain energy of the brain. This energy can also manifest movement by causing small fires, even producing objects or animals falling from the sky.

GHOSTS, WRAITHS, AND BANSHEES MESSENGERS

Less common, especially in the United States, are messenger ghosts, wraiths, and banshees. When these types of ghosts appear, it is usually considered a bad omen and a messenger of death. On one occasion, a black cat has appeared in the White House as an omen of death to come.

GEOLOGY

There are many different theories on why and how ghosts manifest; one such theory is the connection between ghosts and geology. Such geological formations could be faults, including the Tectonic Strain Theory, radon gas, subsurface water and rivers, and types of rock, including granite. Many paranormal investigators are now looking at what the geological makeup is and seeing if there is a connection between what the ground is telling them and what is going on in the area.

Washington State is full of settlements that bloomed from the mining industry. The towns are built above the mines that yielded silica, gold, and many other ores such as quartz, which is a highly charged mineral. Many paranormal researchers believe that the energy and memories of past spirits can be held in the crystalline rock types such as silica, quartz, and granite. Numerous buildings, which have reported a haunting, are built out of quarried stone full of quartz deposits.

Now that you know a little more about hauntings and ghosts, I invite you to jump in your vehicle or cozy up in your favorite chair and take a journey into Washington's Haunted Hotspots.

VANCOUVER TO CENTRALIA

Beginning Directions: From Interstate 5 head East on East Mill Plain Boulevard, turn right at East Reserve Street.

FORT VANCOUVER

612 East Reserve Street, Vancouver, WA 98661
www.nps.gov

Fort Vancouver was christened with a bottle of rum in 1825 as a hopeful beginning to the Hudson Bay Company. By 1829, the company moved the fort closer to the Columbia River, and by 1860, the Hudson Bay Company abandoned the fort and moved north, closer to the Canadian border. The U.S. Army stepped in and used it as storage and living quarters; by 1861, only fifty people resided at the fort and in 1866, a large fire broke out burning down most of the fort. The fort was rebuilt and became a bustling center of activity during WWI and WWII. After two wars, the fort was shut down for good.

Many notable United States officers were stationed at Fort Vancouver early in their careers, including Generals Ulysses S. Grant, George B. McClellan, Phillip Sheridan, William T. Sherman, Omar Bradley, and George Pickett. Now, most of the fort buildings are either businesses or preserved museums, and the rest of the fort is preserved as a living museum.

Officers Row is thirty-four residential units and office space, including the Grant, Marshall, and Howard Houses. Many ghostly reports from visitors, residents, and employees of these stately Victorian buildings circulate. Icy fingers touch people, telephones ring that are not plugged in or are off the hook. In one house, freshly brewed coffee has been known to disappear. Do ghosts drink coffee? One business on Officers Row reports the fax machine continually becomes tuned into a religious radio station thatt blares holy voices out of its speakers.

THE GRANT HOUSE RESTAURANT

1101 Officers Row, Vancouver, WA 98661
(360) 696-1727

The Grant House is named after President Ulysses S. Grant, after he was stationed at the fort in the 1850s as a quartermaster. Grant returned to the fort as a visitor after serving two terms as president in 1879. Grant never officially stayed in the house, but may have frequented it during his commission as a young officer. The Grant House is part of Officers Row and was the first house constructed. After its run as a home ended, the house was turned into an officers' club and today is a restaurant. A ghost named Sully has been heard and felt by the employees. On one occasion, a patron to the restaurant reported seeing a man looking out the second story window.

DR. JOHN MCLOUGHLIN HOUSE

(next to Dr. Forbes Barclay House)
719 Center Street, Vancouver, WA 98661

The Dr. John McLoughlin House was the primary residence for the Chief Factor of the fort. Dr. John McLoughlin lived in the house during his tenure until a forced retirement in 1845 where he homesteaded in Oregon City. His home was saved from demolition and moved to its current location in 1909. The house is a restored replica of how Dr. McLoughlin would have lived. The graves of the Doctor and his wife, Marguerite, are next to his house. Some say he has come back to visit; heavy footsteps are heard and glowing mists are reported in the house and outside near the Parade Grounds.

ARMY BARRACKS

The old army barracks are built over colonial gravesites but may not be the only reason they are haunted. Fort Vancouver served as the departmental headquarters and transportation center for moving the Buffalo Soldiers throughout the Pacific Northwest. The old barracks were home to these Buffalo Soliders; many ended their careers at the fort and several more are buried in the grounds, including one who drowned in a nearby pond in 1899. The barracks are still used by the past tenets as well as the current residents. The unseen tenets enjoy playing tricks on the current residents of the old Veterans Hospital. Employees relate stories of locking doors only to find them unlocked a few hours later, windows are found open in the middle of winter when no one has been in the building.

The Old Veterans Hospital is best known for the heart wrenching screams which can still be heard from the patients. The third floor, which housed the mental patients, is especially active with unusual phenomena. Rumors circulate that in a certain room on the third floor of the hospital, if paper is present, it will float to the ceiling, and when the paper is removed from the ceiling, it will float up again until taken out of the room.

Directions from Fort Vancouver to Hazel Dell Park: Head North on East Reserve Street toward East Evergreen Boulevard; turn left at East Mill Plain Boulevard; take a slight right to merge onto I-5 toward Seattle; take exit 3 for NE Hwy 99; merge onto WA-99 turn right at NE 68th Street.

HAZEL DELL PARK

2300 Northeast 68th Street, Vancouver, WA 98665

The park encompasses twenty acres including a wooded area. Two little boys are said to play in the woods here; if you see them, they stop and look at you, then slowly fade away.

They enjoy following visitors around the park and tend to give you the feeling of dread and that you need to leave urgently.

Even during daylight hours, if you wander into the woods, you may experience a feeling that you need to leave promptly or you may even see the two boys.

Directions from the Hazel Dell Park to Buzz's Sports Bar & Grill: Head East on NE 68th Street toward NE 27th Avenue; turn left at NE St. Johns Road; turn right at NE 119th Street; turn left at NE 117th Avenue, turn right at West Main Street; turn right at SE Clark Avenue; turn left at SE 1st Street.

BUZZ'S SPORTS BAR & GRILL

705 SE 1st Street, Battleground, WA 98604

Located in historic downtown Battleground, past employees of the former restaurant and bar claim to have had many out-of-the-ordinary experiences. One former employee claims to have caught one of the spirits on film, while others only experienced noises.

Bartenders claim televisions are turned on after closing and locking up the building for the night. Boxes would fall off shelves in the freezer area and other items have been known to move around on their own. As this story is written, Buzz's Bar and Grill is closed and it is unknown what is going to fill the empty building.

Directions from Buzz's Sports Bar & Grill to Monticello Middle School: Head West on SE 1st Street toward SE Clark Avenue, turn right at SE Clark Avenue, turn left at E Main Street, continue on NE 219th Street; turn left at NE 10th Avenue, turn right onto ramp to I-5 towards Seattle, take exit 36, merge onto WA-432 W towards WA-4 W, turn left at Hemlock Street, turn right at 28th Avenue.

MONTICELLO MIDDLE SCHOOL

1225 28th Avenue, Longview, WA 98632

A young girl was taking cookies to the construction workers building at the new middle school when she slipped and fell into wet cement. As she laid face down, unconscious in the cement, she unfortunately was not discovered, and suffocated to death.

The young girl has been seen wandering the hallways of the school. Students and staff of the middle school have heard the faint sound of humming. Some students even claim the sounds of footsteps follow them to their classes.

Sightings: Spirit Lake

Spirit Lake, WA 98648

Men often go missing after hunting elk near Spirit Lake. Local Indians tell stories of ghost elk that wander the shores luring men in close enough to the lake for Seatco (the resident lake monster) to grab them and drag them under the water. Seatco victims' voices are now heard echoing from the depths of the lake.

 **Directions from Monticello Middle School to Frosty's Saloon and Grill:** Head South on 28th Avenue toward Hemlock Street, turn left at Hemlock Street, turn left at Nichols Boulevard, turn right at WA-4 turn left at West Cowlitz Way, turn left at North Kelso Avenue, turn left to merge onto I-5 towards Seattle, take exit 71 for WA-508 East toward Onalaska, turn left at Forest Napavine Road East, turn right at East Stella Street, turn left at 2nd Avenue NE, turn right at West Washington Street, turn left at East Front Avenue.

Frosty's Saloon and Grill

113 West Front Street, Napavine, WA 98565

Located in the city of Napavine, Frosty's is an old saloon which was established in the early 1900s. The Napavine's settlers started arriving in the 1850s, and many of its residents found work as loggers. By 1913, the town was established enough to be incorporated and the Frosty's building was one of the first hangouts frequented by the loggers in the area.

Patrons of the saloon report activity caused by a ghostly logger. Cold spots and electronic disturbances remain unexplained in the building.

Directions from Frosty's Saloon and Grill to The Olympic Club Hotel: Head northwest on East Front Avenue toward West Washington Street, turn right at West Washington Street, turn left at 2nd Avenue East, continue on Rush Road, turn left to merge onto I-5 toward Seattle, take exit 81 for Mellen Street, turn right at Mellen Street, turn left at South Tower Avenue.

Patrons report seeing a ghostly logger saddling up to the bar at Frosty's Saloon & Grill.

THE OLYMPIC CLUB HOTEL AND THEATER, THE OLYMPIC CLUB PUB, THE NEW TOURIST BAR

112 North Tower Avenue, Centralia, WA 98531
(360) 736-5164 △ (866) 736-5164 △ www.mcmenamins.com
Sunday through Thursday 7am - 12 Midnight
Friday and Saturday 7am - 1am

Buried bodies, prostitutes, bootleggers, corrupt police, and a robber or two—the Olympic Club has it all, including ghosts. The famous mail robber and notorious escape artist Roy Gardner was captured on June 16, 1921 in the hotel. Trying to elude police, he bandaged his face so he would not be recognized. The landlady, worried he might have a contagious disease, summoned the police. After a doctor was brought in to remove the bandages, his identity was discovered and he was arrested.

Guests see a ghostly man standing by the cast-iron stove at the Olympic Club Hotel, Pub, Theater, and The New Tourist Bar.

A tunnel was found that led from the bar under the train station to a house across the way. Is this how the bar stayed afloat during prohibition?

In the basement, a pickle barrel is still intact that reveals a false bottom and trapdoor. When the train station behind the building replaced its platform, a forgotten body was found.

Rumors persist that the police chief of Centralia ran the poker games while his wife was in charge of the brothel upstairs. You can still see his motorcycle sidecar that he lost during one of his poker games.

In 1906, a resident of a former hotel on the site was trapped in his room as the hotel burned to the ground. Panicking, he jumped out of the window; his injuries were so extensive he died a few months later.

No one knows how many spirits remain in these buildings. Sometimes, a man is seen standing by the large cast-iron stove in the bar. Chairs move by an invisible hand and sometimes laughter can be heard in the Pub area. One night a manager was closing up for the evening and, after extinguishing all the candles, he left the room to close up another area. Upon returning, he found all the candles relit.

Guests of the hotel sometimes hear women crying. Were these cries from a prostitute? Doors open and close and you just never know what you are going to experience—maybe even an apparition.

Sightings: Oakville Raining Blobs

Oakville, WA 98568

August 1994, the town of Oakville experienced a different kind of rain. It wasn't water; it seemed to be some sort of jelly substance. With a population of 665, a flu epidemic soon hit caused by the strange rain that fell more than six times on the small town, blanketing some twenty square miles. The residents were sick from three weeks to three months.

Washington State Department of Health examined the substance and found white human blood cells and bacteria that made its home in the digestive system.

The residents wondered where this could have come from. There were reports of black helicopters and airplanes flying unusually low over the town weeks and days prior to this down pour of jelly; the United States Air Force denies any involvement with this rain.

Could it be waste from an airplane? Any waste would be dyed blue and this was a clear substance.

Whatever it was left a lasting mystery on the small town, and in 1997, the substance showed up in a parking lot in Everett.

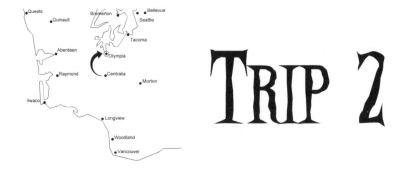

TRIP 2

OLYMPIA AREA

Beginning directions: From Interstate 5 exit 105 toward 14th Avenue SE, keep left to stay on the 14th Avenue SE, left at Washington State Capital.

GOVERNOR'S MANSION

Capital Hill - Olympia, WA 98508
(next to the John L. O'Brien Building)
(360) 586-Tour △ www.wagovmansion.org

In 1908, the Washington State Governor's Mansion was built, but as grand as the house was, it was very uncomfortable to live in. By 1915, Governor Lister moved his family out; he said it was just too expensive to heat and the house was too cold to live there further.

The mansion was plagued with problems. The roof leaked, faulty plumbing, and sagging floors were just the tip of the iceberg, but the mansion lasted through it all—even talk of demolition. Governor Daniel J. Evans' wife finally had the mansion remodeled, and since then, it has been turned into the comfortable showplace it was always meant to be.

The mansion has housed the governors and their families; some of which have stayed. Three governors have passed away while still in office and who knows how many just hang around! The house is open to tours and some guests have seen more than just the governor's house. Several people have seen a boy wearing a sailor suit, riding a tricycle, and other guests have heard the sounds of a ball bouncing in the hallway.

Governor's Mansion.

When the mansion was remodeled in the 1970s, the boy riding the tricycle seemed to have quieted down and hasn't been seen since. The sound of the bouncing ball is sometimes still heard, though.

Direction from the Governor's Mansion to the Bigelow House Museum: Head East on 4th Avenue toward N Washington Street, turn left at E Bay Drive NE, turn right at Glass Avenue NE.

BIGELOW HOUSE MUSEUM

918 Glass Avenue NE, Olympia, WA 98506
(360) 753-1215 △ www.bigelowhouse.org
Memorial Day through Labor Day
Saturday - Sunday 12pm - 4pm
Open for tours year round by appointment.

Built in the 1850s by the Territorial Legislator and lawyer Daniel Bigelow, the Bigelow house is the oldest wooden residence in Olympia and one of the oldest in the Pacific Northwest. Mr. Bigelow had his hands full; he was a father to nine children in addition to his regular job as the Thurston County

Bigelow House is where the spirit of Mr. Bigelow still goes on about his daily business.

prosecution attorney, probate judge, territorial auditor, city councilman, Olympia postmaster, and superintendent of schools—all at once.

Mr. Bigelow died in 1905 and his wife followed him in 1926. The house has remained a residence and in the Bigelow family until in 1994, when it was sold to the Bigelow House Preservation Association and opened as a museum.

The Bigelow family still resides in the house on the second floor—as well as the original Mr. Bigelow. He has been seen all about the house tending to his many jobs and always watching over his children and his home, which he built for his wife and family so many years ago.

Directions from the Bigelow House Museumto Old High School Gym: Head west to Glass Avenue NE toward Pear Street NE, turn left at East Bay Drive NE, turn left at 4th Avenue, slight right at Pacific Avenue SE, at Golf Club Road SE take the 3rd exit onto Lacey Boulevard SE, at Homann Drive SE take the 2nd exit onto Pacific Avenue SE, at traffic circle take 2nd exit onto Pacific Avenue, turn right at 4th Street, turn left at S Peterson Street.

Old High School Gym

340 Peterson Street South, Roy, WA 98580
www.cityofroywa.us
The gym is available to rent special events

In the town of Roy, the elementary school stands where the original high school once stood. All that remains of the high school after a devastating fire in the 1950s is the gymnasium.

Residents to Roy report that the old gym emits a spooky feeling and cold spots are abundant all over the building. The locker room lies frozen in time, untouched since the school burned. Sounds of lockers opening and shutting echo from this room and some visitors have heard whispers and footsteps from the game viewing area above the court.

Directions from the Old High School Gym to Paradise Inn: Head South on South Peterson Street toward 4th Street, turn right at 4th Street, turn left at McNaught Road South, turn left at WA-702, turn right WA-7, continue on WA-706.

PARADISE INN

Paradise, Mount Rainier National Park, WA 98329
(360) 569-2275 △ www.rainier.guestservices.com

Located in Mount Rainier National Park, the 1917 Paradise Inn opens for the summer months.

Employees have heard furniture moving in the pre-season setup. They have also heard someone strolling the hallways and rooms above the Annex part of the Inn. You get the feeling of being watched when you are all alone and the wind turns into voices as it blows through the dormer windows.

Climbers who have stayed at the inn have later died while climbing the mountain terrain. Many are thought to stay on at the inn terrifying employees and guests.

SIGHTINGS: MOUNT RAINIER

Mount Rainier, WA

Naturally heated cavities in the mountain are said to be home to an alien base. Since the mid 1940s, a constant stream of UFO sightings have been reported around the mountain.

The mountain is also said to hold the records of the lost civilization of the Lemurians, an ancient alien/reptilian race that is the Pacific's answer to Atlantis. In fact, claims have been made that an extraterrestrial race from Atlantis known as Kumaras, were the leaders in the Lemurian civilization.

Mount Rainier 14,410 feet.

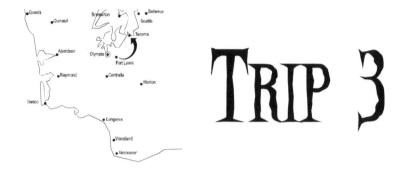

TRIP 3

FORT LEWIS TO TACOMA

Beginning Directions: From Interstate 5 exit 41st Division Drive.

FORT LEWIS

Fort Lewis, WA 98433

Fort Lewis is one of the largest and most requested duty stations in the United States. Named after Meriwether Lewis of the Lewis and Clark Expedition, it first started out as Camp Lewis in 1917.

The woods north of Fort Lewis Road are known to have been the site where motorists have seen spirits walking in the woods. They have been spotted looking transparent and slightly glowing wearing clothing from the nineteenth century. Reports of a mysterious cloaked figure walking near the road have been mentioned for more than a hundred years. The Steilacoom tribe is still making their home in the woods, and more than 600 Indians occupied this land before the English settled in the area.

The Fort Lewis Inn and Museum has had reports of disturbances, from not only military personnel but also motorists on the I-5 freeway. Lights are mysteriously turned on and off, reports that the alarm has been triggered at night; when investigated the alarm remains intact and no one is found. Doors open and shut by themselves as well as mysterious shadows that have also been seen looking out the windows.

In the North Fort Lewis Old Barracks a former cleaning lady claims that doors would slam and the cleaning carts would roll by themselves down the hallways. Reports of platoons running and singing cadences have been heard in the early morning hours, upon investigation no one is seen.

SIGHTINGS: UFO AT FORT LEWIS

In the late 1960s, an ex-solider claims to have seen between three and five small orbs of light debark from a larger ship over Fort Lewis. After basic training had been dismissed, the group of fifteen men saw the orbs while waiting to use the telephones. An ex-army soldier claims the orbs flew out of sight at tremendous speeds, and within a few minutes, returned to the larger craft and disappeared.

Directions from Fort Lewis to Thornwood Castle: head north on I-5 exit Thorne Lane, keep left at the fork follow signs for Tillicum, turn left at North Thorne Lane SW.

THORNEWOOD CASTLE

8601 North Thorne Lane SW, Lakewood, WA 98498
(253) 584-4393 △ www.thornewoodcastle.com

Most famous for its role in the movie *Rose Red*, Thornewood Castle has its own spirits. Chester Thorne, his wife, Anna, their son, and a small child have all been observed in the house. Chester Thorne likes to unscrew the light bulbs and turn the lights on and off. His wife, Anna, is seen at the window of her room looking down at the gardens.

Some brides admiring themselves on their wedding day in Anna's original mirror have seen her reflection, sitting in the bay window watching them prepare for their big day. When they turn to look, the brides are always alone.

Anna and Chester's son shot himself in the house and his ghost is seen in the gun closet. A grandchild of a former owner is seen playing by the pond on a frequent basis, which is where the child drowned one day.

Chester Thorne built Thornewood Castle in 1911; he hired famed architect Kirkland Cutter to design the 27,000-square-foot mansion. Stained glass from the twelfth century and crystal windows shipped from England adorn the English Tudor/Gothic mansion. In the past, the house had been turned into apartments where the tenents were never alone.

Ghost stories run rampant in this house and on the grounds. Guests and visitors say they have captured some of the spirits on film and have even been followed home.

Make a reservation and maybe you will bump into one of the ghosts or take home more than a memory. This is a private residence that sometimes operates as a Bed and Breakfast. They occasionally open the house to visitors. On the Web site, you may find events scheduled and times when the house will be open. You cannot see the house from the street and it is in a private, gated community.

Directions from Thornwood Castle to McCord Air Force Base: Head east on North Thorne Lane SW toward Union Avenue SW, turn left to merge onto I-5 N, take exit 125 Bridgeport Way, turn right at Bridgeport Way SW, continue on Main Street, turn right at D Street, turn left at 8ᵗʰ Street.

McCord Air Force Base

McCord Air Force Base, WA 98499

McCord Air Force Base hangars the C–141 cargo plane that transported the bodies from the Jonestown massacre. Jim Jones was the leader of the Peoples Temple, a religious cult that was the toast of San Francisco only two years prior to its downfall. In the summer of 1977, migration to the newly-founded Jonestown in Guyana began with more than a thousand residents by 1978. The residents, men, women, children, and the elderly were worked twelve hours a day, six days a week. They lived in little shacks with little nourishment. If a person tried to leave or committed a crime, several punishments were implemented, including drugs, and solitary confinement in a box. Children and some adults called Jim Jones *Dad* or *Father* and the children were surrendered to communal care.

After complaints from many of the relatives of cult members, Congressman Leo Ryan went to Jonestown to investigate. During the first day of his visit to the compound, a member of the cult threatened his life. He decided to cut his trip short and return to the United States with a few of the many members that wanted to leave; as they boarded the plane, Jones' guards opened fire and killed most of the group. That night, Jones laced a fruit-flavored drink with cyanide, sedatives, and tranquilizers, then proceeded to force the members of his group to drink the concoction. For the members who would not drink the concoction, guards were ordered to shoot them; 912 followers died, including 276 children. Jones then shot himself.

In the hanger at McCord where the plane sits, sounds are heard of whispers, and footsteps walking about. Reports of power failures in the hanger are common with no earthly explanation for the phenomenon.

Are these the voices and acts from the unfortunate victims of Jonestown still trying to escape Jim Jones?

Directions from McCord Air Force Base to Steilacoom: Head northwest toward Tuskegee Airman Avenue, turn right at Tuskegee Airman Avenue, turn left at Main Street, continue on Bridgeport Way SW, turn left at McCord Drive SW, turn left at Pacific Highway SW, turn left at Gravelly Lake Drive SW, turn left at Washington Boulevard SW, slight right at military Road SW, turn left at Worthington Street, continue to Main Street.

STEILACOOM

Steilacoom was once the fastest growing town on the Puget Sound, incorporated in 1854 to the Washington territory. Steilacoom had the first Protestant Church north of the Columbia River, the first jail, and the first public library.

In 1873, the Northern Pacific Railroad built its terminal in Tacoma, thus moving the hub of activity out of Steilacoom. Soon the electric trolley was running to the beachside town; hope arose that the town could become a prosperous resort town. Several years later, the railroad did come to town, but located the tracks along the shoreline, cutting the town off from the beach and crushing any hope of a seaside resort town.

Nowadays, Steilacoom is the ferry terminal for Ketron, Anderson, and McNeil Islands, as well as the site of the famous Western State Asylum, where Francis Farmer had her speculated lobotomy. Unfortunately, the remains of the asylum buildings were recently torn down for safety reasons, but you can still visit the cemetery. Steilacoom is also home to three buildings on the National Register of Historic Sites.

THE BAIR DRUGSTORE

1617 Lafayette Street, Steilacoom, WA 98388

The Bair Drugstore was built in 1895, and this building was originally a pharmacy, soda fountain, hardware store, and post office for the town of Steilacoom. W. L. Bair ran this business, and some say he still does.

Each night around seven, forgotten diners come for dinner. Reports of silverware clinking and dinner conversations are heard. The haunting

A ghostly dinner takes place around seven each night at the Bair Drugstore.

includes a gentleman who has been spotted lounging by the wood stove. A woman has been seen in the mirror behind the counter. Jars and other items are known to fly off shelves as well as objects in the building often being found in different spots or just go missing all together. Electronics fail with no good excuse for the malfunction, and drawers also open and close on their own accord. One spirit likes to hang out in the ladies room and another spirit calls out names.

E.R. ROGERS HOUSE

1702 Commercial Street, Steilacoom, WA 98388

In 1852, Edwin R. Rogers, a seaman and merchant, relocated to Steilacoom from a life at sea. A few years later, he married Catherine and soon built a 4,582-square -foot, seventeen-room mansion in 1891 for his new bride and stepdaughter. Unfortunately, in 1893, the Rogers family lost their riches due to economic hardship and moved out of the home they loved so much.

The next owner, Charles Herman, turned the house into a summer guesthouse. In the 1920s, W. L. and Hattie Bair, owner of the Bair drug

Police dogs have refused to enter the E.R. Rogers House after the security alarms have been triggered.

store, and who also ran the post office, bought the house and converted it into a rooming house.

By 1960, the house became vacant; a development company bought it and renovations were made. The building then opened as a restaurant in 1978, and only recently closed its doors.

Many ghosts have been reported, especially because of the deaths that occurred in the house. A former owner's wife killed herself in there, a young girl committed suicide in one of the upstairs rooms, and some say that an American Indian was unjustly hung from a locust tree in the southwest corner of the property.

Alarms are triggered when the restaurant is locked up for the night. A police dog was brought to the restaurant to investigate the unseen burglar, but the dog refused to enter the building. Other electronics have been known to turn on and off by themselves. An apparition of a woman in white has appeared to the staff and patrons alike. Tableware has moved and actually flew across the rooms on several occasions.

The mansion currently has been turned into offices.

FERRY TRAIN TRACKS

66 Union Avenue, Steilacoom, WA 98388

The Ferry Train Tracks are notorious for ghost encounters. You can sometimes hear a faint sound of a ghostly train whistle, then a distinct scream of a person having been struck by the train.

Joshua Bates cow's spirit has been seen walking along the tracks as well. The tale is said to be that Joshua's only possession was a cow. He was well known in the little town and the cow was allowed to wander, freely grazing where it liked.

One day, the cow went missing and Bates heard that a man, Andrew Byrd, took the cow. Enraged, Bates drew a pistol and shot Byrd when he refused any knowledge of his missing cow. In his dying breath, Byrd asked the growing mob not to prosecute Bates; but they could not honor this wish. After a few drinks, the vigilante mob rushed into the jailhouse where Bates was being held for trial and drug the man to a local tree, hanging him without a trial.

The next day, the cow was found wandering near the train tracks by the pier. Bates has been seen wandering the streets of Steilacoom, possibly looking for his lost cow.

The ferry pier is said to have strange occurrences itself. Late at night, a young child can be seen from a distance playing along the pier. When you walk towards the child it will slowly mature into a much older and feeble-looking figure, until it slowly fades away.

Train tracks directly in front of the pier are also known as the Fairy Tracks.

 # SIGHTINGS: WHE-ATCHEE

A female lake monster called Whe-atchee inhabits Lake Steilacoom.

Whe-atchee is known to attack locals who come to the lake for recreation. Nisqually Indians will not fish or swim in the lake. Lake Steilacoom was created in 1853 when a dam was built across Chambers Creek for a sawmill and a grist mill.

Directions from Steilacoom to the Tacoma Orphanage: Head northeast on Lafayette Street toward Balch Street, continue on Chambers Creek Road, turn right at 64th Street West, slight left at 67th Avenue West, turn right at Cirque Drive West, continue on South 56th Street, turn left at S Tacoma Way, turn right to merge onto South Union Avenue, turn left at South Center Street, turn right at South Adams Street.

TACOMA ORPHANAGE

2911 S Adams Street, Tacoma, WA 98409

The Tacoma Industrial Home burned down a century ago but some of the children who lived there still hang around.

The land the orphanage sat on is now a youth center. Youth group children claim hearing crying in one of the buildings from the ghostly children. The adult employees have seen children playing in the yard and around the building.

Directions to Point Defiance Park from Tacoma Orphanage: Head south on South Adams Street toward South 31st Street, turn left at South Union Avenue, turn left onto the WA-16 W, take exit 3 for 6th Avenue toward WA-163 N/Ruston, turn right at North Pearl Street.

POINT DEFIANCE PARK

5400 North Pearl Street, Tacoma, WA 98407
(253) 591-5339 △ www.metroparkstacoma.org
Please check website for events, times, and prices.

Late in the 1980s, a twelve-year-old girl was murdered in Point Defiance Park. Her body was later discovered in the shrubbery, but her killer was never caught.

Some nights you can hear the sounds of a bicycle along Five Mile Drive. Visitors have seen her peddling the bike along the road; when they take a second look, she has disappeared. Ghostly footsteps and crying have also been heard along the drive.

Visitors hear ghostly footsteps at The Pagoda.

THE PAGODA

5801 Trolley Lane, Tacoma, WA 98407
(253) 305-1010

The Pagoda was built as a replica of a seventeenth-century Japanese Lodge. Opening in 1914 as a waiting room for streetcars, it is now rented out for special events.

Visitors to the Pagoda sometimes hear footsteps walking down the stairs on the east side of the building after dark. Sighing can be heard and cold spots in the storage area are a very common occurrence.

It is said a man waiting for his wife to return from Vashion Island witnessed her drowning when her dingy capsized. Each week, the couple would ride the trolley; she would then board a dingy for the mainland to visit her parents. Each week, her husband would wait at the Pagoda for her to return. After watching her small boat overturn and her heavy skirts pull her under the water to her death, he could no longer go on

30

without his love, and the distraught husband walked down to the bathroom and shot himself.

FORT NISQUALLY

Travel back in time and maybe see a few ghosts, too. In 1833, The Hudson Bay Company established the first European settlement on the Puget Sound. This fort became a bustling center for trade.

Today, Fort Nisqually is a living history museum. Two original buildings are preserved, the Factor House built in 1854 and the Granary built in 1851.

Many tourists have seen an old ghostly man sitting on the front porch of the Factor House. The old man is also known to sometimes take a walk in the evenings around the grounds of the fort.

Directions from Point Defiance Park to the Old City Hall: WA-163, turn left at N 51st Street (turns right and becomes Gallagher Way), continue on Ruston Way, North Schuster Pkwy, turn right at South 7th Street, and turn right at Commerce Street.

A ghostly man has been seen walking near Fort Nisqually Museum.

OLD CITY HALL

625 Commerce Street, Tacoma, WA 98402

Tacoma City Hall is home to a wide variety of ghostly activity. The spirits ride the elevators, turn the lights on and off, and lock and unlock doors. Built as the county jailhouse and police station, rumors of executions and hangings that went on are still persistent. Criminals still haunt the building and some are even still in their jail cells.

The city offices have since moved to a modern location but the ghosts remain. The chimes in the tower still ring even now after they have been removed. Police often are called out to the old building after the security alarms and fire alarms go off for no reason. Some security guards do not last long, frustrated with the pranks the spirits like to play. Doors that are secured are often found unlocked later; others tell stories of lights turning on in one room and, as you approach, the light will turn off and turn on in another room.

Built in 1893, the brick walls at the base of the building are eight feet thick and are made with bricks from the ballast of ships. The

Security guards quit suddenly after being tormented by the ghosts at Tacoma Old City Hall.

clock tower is a freestanding structure and in 1905 was fitted with chimes. The building was abandoned in 1959 after the city offices were relocated. After being vacant for ten years, a company bought the building and renovated it into restaurants and shops. Businesses failed and again the building was up for sale. A company bought it with the hopes of turning it into condos.

After some setbacks the building is up for sale again.

Directions from the Old City Hall to University of Puget Sound: South on Commerce Street toward South 7th Street, turn left at South 7th Street, turn left at Pacific Avenue, continue on South Schuster Pkwy, continue on North 30th Street, turn right at North Union Avenue, turn left at North 15th Street.

UNIVERSITY OF PUGET SOUND

1500 N Warner Street, Tacoma, WA 98416

Some say that the serial killer Ted Bundy may have killed his first victim at the University of Puget Sound and dumped her body near a building that was in the middle of construction at the time. After graduating from Woodrow Wilson High School in Tacoma, Bundy was awarded a scholarship to the University of Puget Sound. After only two semesters, Bundy transferred to the University of Washington in Seattle.

Over the years, students report seeing a young girl with long, straight hair walking in the halls of the building near where her body was dumped. Students also report unearthly sounds that cannot be explained coming from somewhere within the building.

The theater was named the Inside Theater until sometime in 1988, when it was renamed Norton Clapp Theater. It is located inside the Jones Hall Building. No one knows who the spirit is that moves scenery around or why it is attached to the theater, but the spirit enjoys terrifying students and employees alike. Slamming doors and making other strange noises are a favorite activity. But not all bad has come from this spirit. On one occasion, a student reports that as she leaned over the catwalk above the stage, she lost her balance and started to fall, when the helpful spirit pulled her back on the catwalk to safety.

33

Sightings: Mysterious Hole

Tacoma, WA

A local newspaper article from the 1980s claims that a mysterious hole in the back yard of a home in Tacoma consumes everything thrown into it. Cavers explored the hole and saw little cone-shaped stones they have never seen before.

One of the earlier owners of the home tells a story of being lowered down the hole only to have his oil lamp sucked out of his hands. Another told of filling the hole with all kinds of items, but the hole spewed the objects back out. Still another owner filled the hole with old tires, but the hole seemed to consume the tires, too, and they soon disappeared from sight.

Directions University of Puget Sound to the Gog-li-hi-ti Wetlands: North on North Union Avenue toward North 16th Street, turn right at North 30th Street, slight right at North Schuster Pkwy, take left ramp onto I-705 S, exit onto I-5 N, exit 136A for 20 Street E, merge onto 33rd Avenue E, turn left at 20th Street E, turn right at Frank Albert Road E, turn right at North Levee Road.

Gog-li-hi-ti Wetlands

**South of the Wetlands Park
North Levee Road West past Frank Albert Road East
Tacoma, WA**

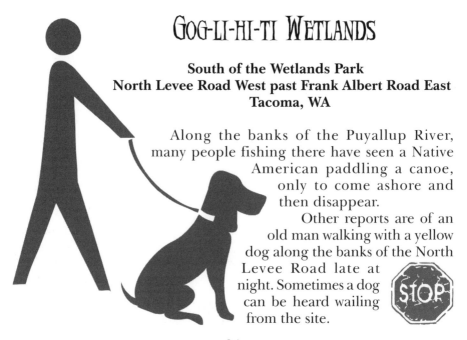

Along the banks of the Puyallup River, many people fishing there have seen a Native American paddling a canoe, only to come ashore and then disappear.

Other reports are of an old man walking with a yellow dog along the banks of the North Levee Road late at night. Sometimes a dog can be heard wailing from the site.

TRIP 4

EAST OF TACOMA CITIES

Beginning Directions: State Highway 512 East, exit Meridian, turn right at 9th Avenue SE.

PUYALLUP FAIRGROUNDS

110 9th Avenue SE, Puyallup, WA 98271
www.thefair.com
Beginning of September for the fair. △ Spring Fair: Mid April.

Built in 1955, standing at fifty-five feet tall, the Ferris Wheel has a ghostly couple that rocks one of the buckets late at night when the wheel seems to come alive and runs on its own.

Directions to from Puyallup Fairgrounds to Pick 'N Shovel Restaurant 'N Lounge: West on 9th Avenue SE toward South Meridian, turn left at South Meridian, turn left to merge onto WA-167 N toward Seattle, exit WA-410 E toward Sumner merge onto WA-410 slight right at WA-165.

35

Pick 'N Shovel Restaurant 'N Lounge. **The former owner is said to follow women to the restroom.**

PICK 'N SHOVEL RESTAURANT 'N LOUNGE

527 Church Street, Wilkeson, WA 98396
(360) 829-6574 △ www.picknshovel.com
Open 7 days a week 9am to last man standing

Several spirits hang around this old bar. A departed past owner is said to follow women to the restroom. He is known to swing the doors near the restroom when you least expect it. Patrons and employees hear dishes and pots clinking in the kitchen and items move to different locations by themselves. Footsteps are heard walking around the bar area and sometimes patrons see darting shadows there.

Directions from the Pick 'N Shovel Restaurant 'N Lounge to Enumclaw Cemetery: Head NW on Wilkeson-Spiketon Road toward Church Street, slight right at WA-165, turn left to stay on WA-165, turn right toward WA-410, turn right at WA-410, turn left at 244th Avenue SE, turn left at SE 416th Street.

ENUMCLAW CEMETERY

23717 SE 416th Street, Enumclaw, WA 98022

Apparitions have been seen wandering the grounds. It is reported that the temperature is always twenty degrees colder inside the cemetery than outside the cemetery gates.

Directions from Enumclaw Cemetery to Black Diamond Cemetery: East on SE 416th Street toward Holy Cross Cemetery, turn left at Black Diamond-Enumclaw Road SE, turn left at Jones Lake Road/Railroad Avenue, stay to the left to Morgan Street.

BLACK DIAMOND CEMETERY

Cemetery Hill Road, Black Diamond, WA 98010
(360) 886-2142 △ www.blackdiamondmuseum.org

Black Diamond was a company town with the workers of the mine being Irish and Welsh, but it soon encompassed a wide variety of nationalities. The miners bought houses in the town and had to pay the Black Diamond Mine for the land the houses sat on. After some labor disputes with the union, many miners lost their jobs and found themselves homeless. Morgantown was funded by the labor union just a few miles away from Black Diamond; the houses were built quickly with little or no insulation. Some of the houses still stand today.

After all the labor settlements between the mine and the union were finalized, a few miners went back to work at the mine, but many were blackballed for life.

On foggy nights in the Black Diamond Cemetery, the glow from lanterns and the whistling of forgotten miners still linger in the air. An apparition of a young lady is seen looking at the grave markers, most likely searching for someone, while others have caught a glimpse of a white horse walking among the headstones.

Directions from Black Diamond Cemetery to Franklin Town Site (Black Diamond Railroad Museum for information on tours) head East on Morgan Street; Morgan Street will turn into Railroad Avenue.

Glowing lanterns have been seen at the Black Diamond Cemetery on foggy nights.

FRANKLIN TOWN SITE

Near town of Black Diamond △ Hanging Gardens State Park
(360) 886-2142 △ www.blackdiamondmuseum.org
Black Diamond Railroad Museum gives guided tours
of the Franklin town site.

Franklin is a coal-mining town from the 1880s. Still frozen in time, you can walk among the foundations of buildings; artifacts are strewn about including the coal that made the town. The primary mine was over 1,000 feet deep. Strange events are known to occur at night.

One story is that several campers in the area packed up in the middle of the night and fled in fright after seeing eerie shadows dart around the ruins. Lights from old-style lanterns illuminate the empty ruins, and sounds of wagons pulled by horses walking down the overgrown roads are heard.

On August 24, 1894, a deadly fire swept through the Oregon Improvement Coal Mine killing thirty-seven miners, many of them buried at the Franklin Cemetery. Legends say that if you throw rocks down the nearby mineshaft, screams will return of the miners' spirits who are still working, believing a cave-in is happening.

Directions from the Black Diamond Railroad Museum to Tahoma National Cemetery: Head south on Jones Lake Road/Railroad Avenue toward Baker Street, turn left at Baker Street, turn left at 3rd Avenue, continue on Maple Valley Black Diamond Road SE, turn left at SE Wax Road, continue on SE 240th Street.

TAHOMA NATIONAL CEMETERY

18600 SE 240th Street, Kent, WA 98042

The only National Cemetery in Washington State, Tahoma covers 158 acres and is the home to more than 15,924 heroes, including Second Lieutenant Barrek, Medal of Honor recipient for action during the American Civil War.

Visitors to the cemetery have claimed of seeing spirits walking among the graves.

Directions from the Tahoma National Cemetery to the Supermall Cinema: Head west on SE 240th Street toward 183rd Avenue SE, turn left at 180th Avenue SE, turn left at SE 256th Street, turn left to merge onto WA-18 W, take the C Street SW exit, turn right at C Street SW, turn right at 15th Street SW, turn right at Market Street, turn left at Supermall Way.

THE SUPERMALL CINEMA

1101 Supermall Way, Auburn, WA 98001
(253) 735-6721 △ www.regmovies.com

A spirit in the projection area likes to turn the movies on and off in theaters two, nine, and seventeen.

Directions from the Supermall Cinema to Auburn Fred Meyer: West on Supermall Way, turn left to stay on Supermall Way, turn right at 15th Street SW, merge onto WA-167 N, exit 15th Street NW, exit toward West Valley Highway, turn right at 15th Street NW, slight right at 15th Street NE, turn right at Auburn Way North.

AUBURN FRED MEYER

801 Auburn Way North, Auburn, WA 98002
(253) 931-5550

Located across the street from the Auburn Pioneer Cemetery, it is no wonder that a ghost or two have taken a liking to the Fred Meyer store. Most of the activity is found in the shoe department. Employees report hearing sounds of shoeboxes being thrown around the stockroom. When they reluctantly go to clean up the impending mess, they find that nothing has been moved.

Both customers and employees have witnessed shoes flying through the air, usually aimed at them.

Directions from Fred Meyer to Kent Historical Museum: Head northeast on Auburn Way North toward 9th Street NE, continue on Central Avenue South, turn right at East Smith Street.

KENT HISTORICAL MUSEUM

855 E Smith Street, Kent, WA 98030
(253) 854-4330 △ www.kenthistoricalmuseum.org
Wednesday through Saturday 12pm - 4pm

Built in 1907, the Bereiter House is rumored to be haunted. Owner of the Covington Lumber Company, Emil Bereiter, soon became the mayor of Kent. His home was used for many of the social functions and networking the mayor would host.

The two upstairs rooms were used as a billiard room and a card room; many docents and visitors to the house report smelling cigar smoke and hearing laughter coming from the upstairs game room.

After his death in 1913, the house would be known for another prominent resident. In the years prior to World War II, a Caucasian woman bought the home and lived there with her wealthy Japanese husband. He was thought to be a Japanese Admiral and to have built secret panels in the home to hide his radio equipment from the Americans. During the war, he was soon forced into an internment camp and never returned to the home. Future residents have never found the secret panels but the rumors still persist about the Japanese Admiral

Kent Historical Museum. Visitors smell cigar smoke while visiting the museum.

who lived in the home. The Bereiter House is now home to the Kent Historical Museum.

Directions from the Kent Historical Museum to East Hill Elementary School: Head east on SE Kent Kangley Road toward Hazel Avenue North, turn left at Hazel Avenue North, turn right at East James Street, continue on South 240th Street.

EAST HILL ELEMENTARY SCHOOL

9825 South 240th Street, Kent, WA 98031

Legends around the town of Kent claim the elementary school is haunted. Children, teachers, visitors, and employees of the school all claim to have seen a man hanging from an area of the stairs. Reports of moaning, whispering, and choking noises have all surfaced through the years from the facility. People claim if you walk the stairs, your hair will stand up on the back of your neck and you sometimes get a choking sensation.

41

Facility of the school hear moans of the resident ghost at the East Hill Elementary School.

Directions from East Hill Elementary School to Des Moines Marina Park: Head west on South 240th Street toward 98th Avenue South, continue on East James Street, turn left at 68th Avenue South, turn right at South Kent-Des Moines Road, turn right at 8th Avenue South, turn left at South 227th Street, continue on Dock Street.

Des Moines Marina Park

22307 Dock Street, Des Moines, WA 98198

On January 8th each year, a young girl named Diana is seen playing on the swing set and walking along the beach.

The Des Moines Marina was where a children's home was once located. The building sat high on the bluff overlooking the marina and the children would regularly play in the creek, playground, and beach below.

Paranormal investigators claim she is seen on other days of the year and not just the day of her death, January 8th.

42

TRIP 5

SEATTLE

Beginning Directions: From State Route 509 exit South 12ᵗʰ Street, head East.

GLENACRES GOLF COURSE

1000 S 112ᵗʰ Street, Seattle, WA 98168
(206) 244-1720 △ www.glenacresgolf.com

It is speculated that the golf course sits on top of an Indian burial ground. With that in mind, the ghost of an Indian dancing had been seen quite often. During the 1940s through the 1960s, hundreds saw him, including police and newsmen. He was also seen on the trail leading to the grounds.

The nine-hole course features 3,060 yards of golf from the longest tees for a par of 36. Designed by George S. Merritt, the course was opened in 1928. It is now a private club.

Directions from Glenacres Golf Course to Kubota Garden: Head east on South 112ᵗʰ Street, slight left at South 118ᵗʰ Street, left at Des Moines Memorial Drive, turn right at South 116ᵗʰ Street, turn left at Tukwila International Blvd., slight right at Boeing Access Road, continue on South Ryan Way, turn right at 51ˢᵗ Avenue South, turn left at South Creston Street, turn left at 55ᵗʰ Avenue South.

43

KUBOTA GARDEN

9817 55th Avenue South, Seattle, WA 98118
www.kubota.org

Many different stories follow this Japanese garden. It is said that one should not visit the garden with an odd number of people; a ghost will become a companion to your group to make it an even number.

Also, puddles that form in the garden are said to be haunted by the blood of ghosts of people who have died there; don't step in them or you will anger the ghosts.

It is rumored another murder happened in the home located in the gardens and the spirit of the murdered person whispers and the wind howls as you go down the path near the house.

Fujitaro Kubota, an emigrant from Japan, bought five acres in 1927, which soon grew to twenty acres. As the owner of the Kubota Gardening Company, Kubota succeeded in displaying the beauty of Japanese gardens in the Pacific Northwest. The gardens were his home, office, and display center. Kubota died in 1973 at the age of ninety-four.

Directions from Kubota Garden to the Museum of Flight: Head south towards Ryan Street, turn right at South Creston Street, turn right at 51st Avenue, turn left at South Ryan Way, continue on Boeing Access Road, turn right at East Marginal Way.

MUSEUM OF FLIGHT

9404 E Marginal Way South, Seattle, WA 98108
(206) 764-5720 △ www.museumofflight.org
Open 7 days a week 10am - 5pm,
1st Thursday of month open until 9pm

Reports of pilots returning one last time to take the controls of their beloved planes are common at this museum. One account is of a woman attending a company party at the museum. She looked up at one of the planes in the main room and saw a man wearing a brown leather flight jacket in one of the cockpits. She looked down to acknowledge a security guard strolling by, and when she looked back up at the plane, the man was gone. She then asked the security guard about the man and he exclaimed that these sightings are common at the museum. If you visit the museum you will see there is no way a man could get into one of the suspended airplane cockpits.

Directions from the Flight Museum to Martha Washington Park: Southeast on East Marginal Way South, slight left at Boeing Access Road, continue on South Ryan Way, turn left at 51ˢᵗ Avenue South, turn left at Rainier Avenue South, turn right at South Myrtle Street, left at Seward Park Avenue South, turn right at South Holly Street, slight left at 57ᵗʰ Avenue South.

MARTHA WASHINGTON PARK

6612 57th Avenue South, Seattle, WA 98115
www.seattle.gov

At the turn of the century, a school was established to house second offense juvenile girls. By the early 1920s and after moving several times, the Martha Washington School finally found a home at Brighton Beach on the shores of Lake Washington.

Rumors claim that, in the 1950s, a janitor went insane and murdered members of the staff and some of the young girls. He dumped the bodies in the lake by the dock before he was finally subdued.

In 1957, the city of Seattle took control of the school and finally closed it in 1971. The buildings are all long gone but part of the dock still remains. The city maintains the site as Martha Washington Park. Visitors to the park claim they hear the cries of women and children late at night. Balls of light floating in the park are common and so are the strange gusts of wind, which seem to come from nowhere.

Directions from Martha Washington Park to Georgetown Castle: North on 57ᵗʰ Avenue South, turn left at South Morgan Street, turn right at Wilson Avenue South, turn left at South Graham Street, turn right at Swift Avenue South, turn left at South Albro Place, turn right at South Eddy Street, turn left at Carleton Avenue South.

GEORGETOWN CASTLE

6420 Carleton Avenue, Seattle, WA 98101

Located in the previous red-light district of Seattle, the three-story turn-of-the century home holds many unexplained secrets and a history clouded in rumors. Peter Gessner was one of the first, if not *the* first, owner of the castle. Gessner ran The Pioneer Square bar, The Central Tavern, and he was well known for his questionable gambling and prostitution activities. Quickly, police started keeping tabs on him, and soon after, he sold the tavern to set up shop in his home outside of Seattle.

Georgetown was a popular location for saloons and brothels after the "war on saloons" started in Seattle. As many as twenty-five saloons, which were open twenty-four hours a day, were established and advertised they had attached lodgings.

Only a year later, Gessner was found dead from apparent suicide in his bedroom. The reports are that he was found in a grotesque contorted position and his gums,

At the Georgetown Castle, an apparition of an old woman wakes guests from their sleep.

tongue, and lips were shriveled and blackened from the carbolic acid he drank.

The next owner was Dr. Willis H. Corson who bought the house in 1912. He was the superintendent and head coroner of the King County Almshouse and Hospital which soon surrounded the property. The hospital was packed with tuberculoses patients, which were set up in a tent city to accommodate the overflow. The hospital was also the crematorium. The Georgetown Castle is rumored to have secret rooms and hallways; a theater is set up in one of the rooms upstairs for entertainment purposes of some sort. One can only imagine the sort of shows that went on in that second-floor room.

An apparition of an old woman wakes up guests from their sleep as she grabs for her throat. Some speculate she is a Spanish woman who went nuts and killed her infant, burying the baby under the back porch. Other stories claim her Spanish lover killed their illegitimate baby and buried the lifeless body under the back porch.

Or was it the story of the servant girl Sarah's infant. Sarah is seen all over the house, in the second-floor stairway, the kitchen, and on the main stairs. A man, possibly Gessner, is seen on the second-story landing pacing and in the bedroom where he was found.

Children's voices and laughter echoes from somewhere on the third floor—are they the children of the prostitutes who once lived there?

Many other strange sights, sounds and events go on daily in the Georgetown Castle. The home is now a beautifully restored private residence, which is opened up occasionally for the Georgetown Art and Garden Walk.

Directions from Georgetown Castle to the Korean Baptist Church: Head north on Carleton Avenue South, turn right at Bailey Street.

KOREAN BAPTIST CHURCH

1201 South Bailey Street, Seattle, WA 98108

Masons built the building, in 1927, as a meeting hall and church. After the Masons moved to larger facilities, the building housed various businesses, but they never stayed in business long. In the 1980s, the

Slamming doors, screams, and shadows have all been reported in the Korean Baptist Church.

47

Korean Baptist Church opened its doors as a school and church in the old building. By 2006, the building was again vacant and in disrepair.

Slamming doors, moans, screams, and shadows have all been reported as happening in the building. This activity could date from the Masons, the Korean Church, or from a plane crash that happened in 1949. A C-46 airplane, upon take-off, had engine failure and crashed down the street, damaging up to eight homes, killing seven people, and injuring a dozen more. Perhaps some of the dead found solace in the old Masonic Temple.

Directions from the Korean Baptist Church to Andy's Diner: Head west on South Bailey Street, turn right onto I-5 N, exit 163 toward Columbian Way, keep left at the fork, follow signs for Spokane Street, keep left at the fork, follow signs for West Seattle Bridge and merge onto Seattle Fwy West, exit onto 4th Avenue South.

ANDY'S DINER

2963 Fourth Avenue South, Seattle, WA 98134

Seven old rail cars were opened in 1947 as a diner in Seattle; it boasted Franklin Roosevelt's Railcar from his re-election campaign in

Andy's Diner. Does the former railcar of Franklin D. Roosevelt hold the spirits of past riders?

Employees smell the rose sent perfume of a former nurse at the Amazon.com Building.

1944. The restaurant was known for the cast of characters who worked there and for its good food.

All of the employees can tell you a ghostly story or two. A bartender reminisced about silverware tossed around and door knobs rattling, lights turning on by themselves, and seeing strange shadows out of the corner of her eye. A waiter tells of seeing an older blond-haired woman walk down the hallway of one of the cars and a busboy tells of an older gentleman with a limp who was never found after entering the cold storage room.

Sadly, this Seattle landmark closed its doors in 2008. The land, which it sits on, is up for sale and its future is unknown at this time—one can only hope it will reopen.

Directions from Andy's Diner to the Amazon.com Building: Head north on 4th Avenue South toward South Forest Street, turn right at South Holgate Street, slight right at Beacon Avenue South, turn left at 14th Avenue South.

THE AMAZON.COM BUILDING

1200 12th Avenue South, Seattle, WA 98144

The Pacific Medical Building on top of Seattle's Beacon Hill is a sixteen-story impressive structure. Built in 1932 by the United States

Government as a Navy/Marine Corps Hospital, the building is most famous for its current resident; it's the headquarters for Amazon.com. The bottom levels house different medical offices and clinics while the upper floors are where Amazon.com is located.

The sixth floor seems to have a lot of supernatural activity according to a former employee of Amazon.com. He recounted stories of janitors repeatedly quitting after one night on the job, security personnel running from the building swearing that objects started levitating off of desks, and, of course, the dead nurse that roams the hallways, calling to anyone she sees to wait for her. You cannot see her; you can smell the rose-scented perfume she used to wear.

The hospital has several passenger elevators, but those are not to be feared. The service elevator is the one that has a terror-filled ride. Security personnel have complained that on many occasions the elevator would get stuck for hours between floors. As they wait for someone to rescue them from their predicament, they can hear people running on the floor and laughing as their names are called out. When security personnel are finally able to get off the elevator, they are always alone on the premises even after the area is thoroughly searched. The sixth floor is said to have been the mental lock-up and the service elevator was the main elevator used to access that floor when the building was used as a hospital.

Directions from the Amazon.com Building to Pier 70: Head north on 12th Avenue South toward South Charles Street, turn left to stay on 12th Avenue South, turn left at Boren Avenue South, turn left at East Yesler Way, turn right at 1st Avenue.

PIER 70

Waterfront Seafood Grill
2801 Alaskan Way △ Pier 70 -Seattle, WA 98121
(206) 956-9171 △ www.waterfrontpier70.com

The employees of the businesses of Pier 70 have reported a ghostly sailor in a pea coat and slouched billed cap hanging around. He is known to enter stores and is seen either out of the corner of an eye or in a mirror. When the employee turns around or maneuvers to better greet the customer, no one is there.

Other reports are the lights turning on and off, as well as toilets flushing by themselves. One employee has reported setting up a large display of glasses only to later hear it come crashing to the floor. When returning to the area to clean it up, there is no sign anything moved or fell.

Employees of the businesses on Pier 70 report merchandise moving on their own.

Ghostly ships have been reported floating out in the harbor by Pier 70; many of the employees claim that the ghost ship is an omen of disaster to come if you see it.

Pier 70 was originally used to store and sort off-loaded fish from local fishing boats. The nearby railroad would then haul the fish to processing plants. Next, it was used as the Washington State Liquor Distribution Center, and by the 1970s, was turned into a mall and later housed a restaurant and disco. When the 1990s arrived, the pier was mainly vacant and run down. MTV renovated part of the pier to become the *Real World House*, Seattle.

The building is now restored and offers restaurants and stores.

Directions from Pier 70 to Underground Seattle: Head southwest on Alaskan Way, left at Marion Street, right at Western Avenue, left at Yesler Way, left at 1st Avenue.

Underground Seattle

608 First Avenue, Seattle, WA 98104
(206) 682-4646 △ www.undergroundtour.com

The town of Seattle was built on mud flats that made for lots of flooding and for toilets that would flush in reverse when the tide was high. After a devastating fire, the city decided it was time to raise the city above the water line. As the town was being rebuilt, the streets were raised, creating the underground city. People would have to climb ladders to go between the upper street level, and to walk on the sidewalk below to enter shops, then climb back up the ladders to cross the street. Once the streets were finished being raised, the underground became storage.

In 1907, the city condemned the underground part of the city due to the bubonic plague. After being closed off, it became a home to gambling, prostitutes, opium dens and the homeless.

The remains of Seattle's underground are still intact as are many of its now-deceased residents: a young miner, an older man, many prostitutes, and a bank security officer have all been "seen" down in the depths.

Directions from the Underground to Seattle Mystery Bookshop: Head north on 1st Avenue toward Cherry Street, turn right on Cherry Street.

SEATTLE MYSTERY BOOKSHOP

117 Cherry Street, Seattle, WA 98104
(206) 587-5737 △ www.seattlemystery.com
Open Monday through Saturday 10am - 5pm
Sunday 12am - 5pm

Seattle Mystery Bookshop is tucked away off Pioneer Square, offering a huge selection of thriller, true crime, and detective books. In the early 1900s, the shop was located a few stores away where a barbershop once operated. The former owner of the barbershop followed the bookstore when they moved to its current location; perhaps he liked the ladies running the store or the selection of books the shop offered. Books fly off shelves and the employees sometimes see a man dressed in early 1900s clothing looking for something to read.

Ask one of the employees about the ghost and they may pull out the picture of the barber next door that likes to hang out at their store.

A ghostly shop owner likes to hang around the Seattle Mystery Bookshop.

Directions from the Seattle Mystery Bookshop to Sorrento Hotel: Northeast on Cherry Street, towards 2nd Avenue, turn left at 7th Avenue, turn right at Madison Street.

SORRENTO HOTEL

900 Madison Street Seattle, WA 98104
(206) 622-6400 △ www.hotelsorrento.com

In the Hunt Club Bar of the Sorrento Hotel, footsteps and moving glasses are a common occurrence. Many guests see a ghostly woman on the fourth floor hallway by room 408.

Directions from the Sorrento Hotel to Pike Place Market: Head southwest on Madison Street toward 8th Avenue, turn right at 7th Avenue, turn left at Seneca Street, turn right at 1st Avenue, turn left at Pike Street.

PIKE PLACE MARKET

1501 Pike Place Market - Seattle, WA 98101
www.pikeplacemarket.org
Ghost tours are available, contact:
(206) 322-1218 or www.seattleghost.com

By the end of 1907, more than ten thousand people a year flocked to the farmers market named Pike Place Market. By 2007, the farmers market hosts 200 year-round commercial businesses, 190 craftspeople, 120 farmers, 240 performers and musicians, and 300 apartment units. "The Market," as the locals like to call it, now serves ten million visitors a year.

The Market is host to several spirits. Princess Angeline, the eldest daughter of the Indian Chief Seattle, lived in a small cabin where the market now sits. Angeline passed away on May 31, 1896. Much loved by Seattle residents, they gave her a grand funeral and laid her to rest at the Lake View Cemetery on Capital Hill. She is seen most often near a wooden column in the center of the lower level and near the Goodwill store.

The ghost of Arthur Goodwin, the nephew of the original developer, has been seen looking down from the Goodwin Library and sometimes playing golf in his office.

The fat lady barber would sing lullabies to her customers in the 1950s. Once asleep, she would rob the men of their money and valuables. In

Pike Place Market has many spirits; the most famous is Princess Angeline, daughter of Chief Seattle.

the 1970s she fell to her death when the floor gave away. You can still hear her sweet lullabies at night.

A little boy, who sometimes visits the Marionettes Puppet Shop, inhabits the Bead Emporium.

Sheila's Magic Shop holds Madame Nora's spirit. She is in the crystal ball that was traded from Pharaoh's Treasure for a scarab. Madame Nora was the proprietor of the Temple of Destiny, a fortune telling shop in the market.

The Greek Deli (Mr. D's) has two spirits that fight in the downstairs freezer, and the Shakespeare and Company bookstore had a book that would not stay on the shelf; the book has since been destroyed. And who knows how many more spirits the market holds?

Directions from Pike Place Market to E. R. Butterworth & Sons Building:
Head west on Pike Place, turn right at Stewart Street turn left at 1st Avenue.

E. R. BUTTERWORTH & SONS BUILDING

1921 First Avenue, Seattle, WA 98101
www.kellsirish.com

This building was one of the earliest morgues for the city of Seattle and is on the National Register of Historic Places. E.R. Butterworth started

A ghostly burial procession has been seen in the E. R. Butterworth & Sons Building.

his mortuary, unknowingly, in Centralia, by selling ready-made caskets in his furniture store during the diphtheria epidemic.

The former Centralia mayor and state legislator moved to Seattle in 1892 and bought an established undertaking business. After a population boom, Butterworth commissioned a four-story building with all the lavish decorations to create the biggest and finest mortuary in Seattle. After the bodies were embalmed, viewed, and had their services, they were taken to the basement to be cremated or to a hearse for a ride to the cemetery. In 1923, Butterworth had outgrown this building and moved his business to 300 E. Pine Street on Capital Hill.

Many businesses have set up shop in the original building, but none have stayed too long. Kells Irish Pub is in the basement where some of the embalming took place and the crematorium was located; access to the pub is on Post Alley.

Frightening reports have been told and retold. A ghostly procession has been seen. Apparitions have arguments and walk through walls and tables. Sometimes, objects disappear and are found months later on a table or windowsill. Wine bottles and tableware fly off counters and shelves. A construction worker saw his tools jump around as if dancing. Doors shake and open on their own accord. One employee saw a coat hanger straighten out and sway back and forth on a doorknob. The reports of activity are endless it would seem.

Directions from E.R. Butterworth Building to Cutters Bayhouse Restaurant:
Head southeast on 1ˢᵗ Avenue toward Stewart Street, turn right at Stewart Street, turn right at Pike Place turn left at Virginia Street.

CUTTERS BAYHOUSE RESTAURANT

2001 Western Avenue, Seattle, WA 98121
(206) 448-4884 △ www.r-u-i.com/cut
Monday through Friday 9:30am - 10pm
Saturday and Sunday 9:30am - 9:30pm

A woman with no face wearing a black dress has been seen near the bar. She is said to approach you, then disappear.

Directions from Cutters Bayhouse Restaurant to the Rivoli: Head northwest on Western Avenue, turn right at Blanchard Street, turn right at 2nd Avenue.

THE RIVOLI

2127 Second Avenue - Seattle, WA 98121

The Rivoli apartment building has had many deaths within its walls. A young Eskimo girl came to Seattle for an improved way of life, but instead, tragically was murdered. She tried to end a romance with a mentally unstable young man; he thought she had been unfaithful and stabbed her in a jealous rage. Her boyfriend then stashed her body in the Murphy bed, paid the next months rent, and fled town. Reports of a foul stench coming from her apartment prompted a search that finally found her rotting corpse.

Residents sometimes will complain of a foul odor in their apartments or in the hallways as well as seeing her apparition. Some unlucky female residents will wake up to the spirit of her murderous boyfriend peering down at them in bed, and coming from her old apartment, a ghostly argument will sometimes reenact itself.

Other spirits have been seen in the apartment building. Two men who contracted AIDS in the early 1980s committed suicide together at the Rivoli. Tenets see them in the hallways and staircase, some locals have seen them looking out of the front doors.

Another ghost is that of an ill woman in her late thirties who had no friends and very few visitors. She used to clog her toilet so the plumber would come and spend time with her. Before her death, social services tried to move her to a hospital for further care, but she would not leave.

Does a young Eskimo girl haunt the Rivoli apartment building?

She still clogs toilets, and if there is any reason for the maintenance man to come to your apartment, she will be there to greet him.

The Real Change office and Action Appliance are the ground floor shops.

Directions from the Rivoli apartments to Hotel Andra: Southeast on 2nd Avenue toward Lenora Street, turn left at Virginia Street.

Hotel Andra

2000 4th Avenue, Seattle, WA 98121
(877) 448-8600 △ (206) 448-8600 △ www.hotelandra.com
Assaggio Restorante is open Monday - Friday Lunch and Dinner,
Saturday Dinner only. Web site has menus that are downloadable.

Roaring music, laughter, and clinking glasses are just a few of the sounds you will hear from a forgotten party in the hotel.

Built in 1926, Hotel Andra opened as an upscale hotel and hosted the upper crust of society parties. Soon, the hotel fell into disrepair and a wide variety of vagrants called it home. In the 1950s, the hotel was renovated and opened as the Claremont Hotel.

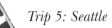
The ninth floor is where many of the unexplained activities have taken place—reports that a worker fell to death from one of the upper floors may be the cause of this activity.

The newly renovated upscale Hotel Andra with 119 rooms is only three blocks from Pikes Place Market.

SIGHTINGS: SUICIDE BRIDGE

State Road 99, across Lake Union, Seattle, WA

The Aurora Bridge in Seattle is well known as the Suicide Bridge. It is also known for the gigantic gnome that sits under the bridge quietly witnessing the deaths of hundreds of people over the years.

Many people see a man and his dog reenact a jump from the bridge as well as other ghostly leaps.

The bridge has been reported as the second deadliest bridge in America only following the Golden Gate Bridge in San Francisco. Built in 1931, the Aurora Bridge is a historical landmark.

The first jumper took his life from the bridge even before it was officially opened in January 1932. He was a shoe salesman. One can only guess the number of jumpers since the bridge was built. Many of the jumpers don't even hit the water but fall onto cars and parking lots and even houseboats. The blacktop has been painted to cover up the blood stains and phones have been installed on the bridge to hopefully help someone who is thinking about jumping. A walking path traverses the entire bridge making it easy to check out.

Directions from Hotel Andra to Jensonia Hotel: Northwest on 4th Avenue toward Lenora Street, turn right at Battery Street, turn left at Aurora Avenue North, Aurora Avenue North turns right and becomes John Street, turn left at 8th Avenue North.

JENSONIA HOTEL

214 8th Avenue, Seattle, WA 98101

The historic hotel has had a long and sordid history. Built in the 1920s, the brick building features seven stories and was host to many lavish parties before it fell into ruins. For many years, the hotel was a drug and prostitution haven. In recent years, the police have cracked down on the area and have cleaned up the hotel, and now, after a renovation, it is now economy apartments.

In early 2003, Lawrence Owens was released from prison and was classified as a level III sex offender. He immediately found residence at the Jensonia only a few apartments away from a young lady with whom he quickly formed a relationship. In the following year, a fire, which consumed the sixth and seventh floors of the hotel, displaced the couple. After securing a residence, Owens urged his girlfriend to move in with him, but when she refused he knocked her to the ground and shot her three times with a shotgun. When the police arrived, he was reloading and aimed the shotgun at several of the officers. They returned fire and Owens died as a result.

The two upper floors are where most of the activity is reported: strange noises, unseen doors open and close, and unexplained balls of light are seen in the hallway and sometimes in the rooms of the old hotel. Did the couple return to their home at the Jensonia Hotel?

Directions from the Jensonia Hotel to the Richard Hugo House: Head south on 8th Avenue North, turn left at John Street, turn right at Westlake Avenue North, turn left at Denny Way, turn right at 11th Avenue.

RICHARD HUGO HOUSE

1634 11th Avenue, Seattle, WA 98122
(206) 322-7030 △ www.hugohouse.org

Built in 1902, the Victorian house has a total of 16,206 square feet. Originally, the building was an apartment house, and then was converted into the Bonney-Watson Mortuary and Funeral Home. After the funeral home closed its doors, the building was turned into a theater, and finally, in 1997, the Richard Hugo organization purchased the building and continues to use the house today. The Richard Hugo House offers support, resources, and a forum for writers to expand their writing skills and to further encourage established writers.

Workers at the house have claimed to have a ghostly presence residing in the basement, perhaps something left over from when the house was used as a mortuary in the 1940s. Several other people have glimpsed shadows moving in different parts of the house.

Directions from the Richard Hugo House to Catalysis Corporation: Head north toward East Olive Street, turn right at East Howell Street, turn left at 16th Avenue, turn right at East John Street.

CATALYSIS CORPORATION

1601 East John Street, Seattle, WA 98112

Built in 1906, the former Capital Hill Methodist Church now holds the headquarters of the Catalysis Corporation.

Some say its past parishioners, the pastor, and his wife haunt the old church. Employees have heard organ music and a forgotten choir practice, sermons are still echoing through the old building, and many cold spots have been reported even on the hottest of days. The Reverend Bagley is seen in the bell tower and on the staircase. His wife, Susannah, is mainly seen with a blue glow around her. She wears a long flowing dress and appears to float. Employees have reported that Susannah speaks with them, usually asking for directions—maybe she is confused since the building has been renovated.

Directions from Catalysis Corporation to the Seattle Museum of Mysteries:
West on East John Street toward 16th Avenue East, turn right at 16th Avenue East, turn left at East Thomas Street, turn right at 15th Avenue East, turn left at East Thomas Street, turn right at Broadway East.

Catalysis Corporation. Employees still see the spirit of the pastor at this former church.

SEATTLE MUSEUM OF MYSTERIES

623 Broadway East, Seattle, WA 98102
(206) 328-6499 △ www.seattlechatclub.org
Call or check Web site for hours and events

The building that houses the Museum of Mysteries is reportedly haunted. The museum itself is downstairs from Aoki Sushi Restaurant.

This museum provides a collection of disturbing information. From The Lost City of Wellington to Bigfoot, it is about everything unknown, including, DB Cooper, crop circles, UFOs, Bruce Lee, Francis Farmer, and much more. A haunted lock-in is offered for the adventurous. They invite you to come and play poker with a ghost, take a ghostly walking tour, or just visit the museum.

Directions from the Museum of Mysteries to the Harvard Exit Theater: Head north on Broadway East toward East Roy Street, turn left at East Roy Street.

THE HARVARD EXIT THEATER

807 East Roy Street, Seattle, WA 98122
(206) 323-8986 △ www.landmarktheatres.com

The Harvard Exit was built in 1924 as the headquarters for the Women's Century Club, founded by Bertha Landis who later became Seattle's first woman mayor. Many of the club's members lived at the residence. When the house was converted into a theater in 1968, reports of ghosts began to surface. Projectors run on their own, film canisters move or disappear, and doors open and cannot be closed without ghostly help.

After a second screen was put in on the third floor in the early 1970s, apparitions started appearing. One such apparition is supposed to be Bertha Landis dressed in 1920s-era style. Another is an unidentified Victorian woman who some speculate may have been strangled in the house or murdered in some other fashion. A man with a mischievous side has also been seen; he likes to play with your hair or clothing, and if you are watching a movie he may play with your popcorn or candy.

Directions from the Harvard Exit Theater to Daughters of the Revolution Building: Head west on Roy Street towards Harvard Avenue.

Daughters of the Revolution Building

800 East Roy Street, Seattle, WA 98102
(206) 323-0600 △ www.rainierchapterhouse.com

The D.A.R building in the Capital Hill district of Seattle was built in 1923, and is a replica of George Washington's Mount Vernon house. Members and guests to the house have witnessed a woman on the stairs dressed in clothing representing the 1800s. Other people have felt as if they walked in on a dance in the ballroom: Some have heard music, some hear the low murmur of a crowd sitting down for dinner or taking a rest from dancing.

The building can be reserved for weddings and other events.

Directions from the Daughters of the Revolution Building to The Grand Army of the Republic Cemetery: Head east on East Roy Street, turn left to stay on East Roy Street, slight left at 10th Avenue East, turn right at East Blaine Street, turn right at East Howe Street.

The Grand Army of the Republic Cemetery

1200 East Howe Street, Seattle, WA 98112

The Grand Army of the Republic Cemetery. You may see the long-dead soldiers from the Civil War walk among the graves.

Next to the Lake View Cemetery is a small civil war cemetery where soldiers in full uniform still walk among the tombstones. Mysterious fogs come out of nowhere, and some have heard the sounds of marching coming from the cemetery grounds.

The Grand Army of the Republic Cemetery was established in 1895. In the following decades, the property went into decline until Seattle's Parks and Recreation took over and turned it into an off-leash dog park.

Recently the Friends of the GAR are taking care of the park. Lake View Cemetery is home to Chief Seattle and his daughter, Princess Angeline, Bruce and Brandon Lee, John Nordstrom, founder of Nordstroms department store, Arthur Denny, and most of the founding Fathers of Seattle.

Visitors to Lake View Cemetery have reported unearthly spirits wandering this cemetery as well.

Directions from The Grand Army of the Republic Cemetery to University of Washington: Head west on Howe Street, turn left at 11th Avenue East, turn right at East Howe Street, turn right at 10th Avenue East, turn left at East Roanoke Street, turn right at Harvard Avenue East, slight right at Eastlake Avenue East, slight left at 11th Avenue NE, turn right at NE 45th Street, turn right at Memorial Way, turn left at Stevens Way, turn left at Pend Oreille Road, turn left at Whatcom Lane.

UNIVERSITY OF WASHINGTON

University of Washington, Seattle, WA 98195

In the Ceramics and Metal Arts Building at the University of Washington Campus, former students at the university have reported different unexplained occurrences. In the intermediate studio area, the sink faucets have turned on by themselves and the pottery wheels have a habit of turning themselves on spontaneously. The senior studio has had reports of the pottery wheels turning on by themselves, but many students have the feeling of being watched when they are alone in the area, too. One student experienced shadows moving when coming in early in the morning. They would dart around the room so fast the papers tacked to the wall would blow up as if a fan were blowing on them. The same student claimed that he once was the first one in the room, turned on the lights, left the room for a few minutes, and upon returning, found all the lights off again.

At the University of Washington Columns Amphitheater, visitors to the park claim to have been run off by a dark spirit who especially likes to target couples who come there to get romantic at night. The spirit will violently shake the closest bush and make a deep frightful growl. If the couple ignores the noise, the spirit will do the same action again more violently and loudly until the couple is frightened and then leaves. Often, visitors who go to the amphitheater will get an uneasy feeling at night. The Columns Amphitheater was so named to recognize that it was the original site of the University of Washington before the university was moved closer to downtown.

Directions from the University of Washington to Green Lake Park: Head southeast on Whatcom Lane, turn left at Pend Oreille Road, turn left at 25th Avenue NE, turn left at NE 65th Street, turn right at NE Ravenna Boulevard, slight right at East Green Lake Drive North.

GREEN LAKE PARK

7201 East Green Lake Drive North, Seattle, WA 98115
(206) 684-4075

David Phillips, who surveyed the area in 1855, named the lake Green Lake due to the abundant amount of algae blooms. The lake was formed from the Vashion Glacier 50,000 years ago and has the maximum depth of thirty feet.

In 1926, the body of Silvia Gaines was found in the lake; she was a prominent young lady who graduated from the prestigious Smith College. Her parents divorced when she was young and she lived back east with her mother. Her uncle was the chair of the King County Board of Commissioners and her father lived in a modest one-bedroom house near Green Lake. After graduation, she headed out west and stayed with her father and his wife. Newspapers of the time state that his wife slept on the couch while the father and daughter slept together in the same bed. When Silvia had enough of the incestuous relationship and wanted to leave and stay with her Uncle, a fight broke out and she was murdered.

In 1927, a boathouse was built with stairs that lead into the lake, and after several swimmers drowned, a lifeguard house was built in the early 1930s. Because of the heavy algae growth, most of the bodies of reported victims were never found.

An aqua theater was erected in the 1950s for the first Seafair. Green Lake hosted such events as the "swimusicals," plays, and jazz festivals, and even had celebrities such as Bob Hope perform at the aqua theater. Ghostly reports are of drowning victims flailing about in the water with silent cries—when the visitors take a second look, there is no one there. For decades, these events were reported to the authorities, but still no bodies were found.

Other reports are that of Silvia Gaines: Is she still trying to get away from her father?

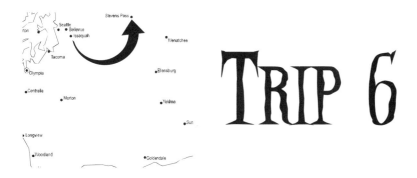

TRIP 6

ISSAQUAH TO STEVENS PASS

SIGHTINGS: MAPLE VALLEY HIGHWAY

Highway 169, Renton, WA

Be careful as you drive down Highway 169 in Renton. An unexplained fog appears on the road. After you pass through the fog, you may see a teenage girl standing alongside of the road crying. Some say she lost her locket after being in a car accident and now is looking desperately for it.

Will she find peace after she finds the locket or maybe she is just trying to catch a ride home. No one knows for sure.

Further down the road is an old abandoned house. Power has long since been disconnected, but through the overgrown shrubs reports of lights being turned on in the rooms are rampant.

Beginning Directions: From Interstate 90 exit 17th Avenue NW, turn right on NW Sammamish Road, turn right on 10th Avenue NW.

THE PICKERING BARN

1730 10th Avenue NW, Pickering Place, Issaquah 98029
(425) 837-3321 △ www.issaquahhistory.org

Issaquah's largest dairy farm for many years, the Pickering farm was purchased by William Pickering in 1867 from earlier homesteaders William and Abbie Castro. The barn was built in 1878, and the dairy barn was added in 1906. The property was later the location for Navy flight training, a base for hang gliders and parachutists, and the barn was used for a court house and a public market. Now the barn can be rented out for weddings and parties.

Abbie and William Castro were killed by a Snohomish Indian attack, and long ago, a young boy drowned in the local creek. Electronic Voice Phenomenon EVPs), Orbs and electrical malfunctions have been reported on the property in and near the barn.

Directions from the Pickering Barn to Carnation Cemetery: Head northeast on 10th Avenue NW, turn right at SE 56th Street, turn right at East Lake Sammamish Pkwy SE, turn left at SE Issaquah-Fall City Road, continue on SE Duthie Hill Road, continue on 292nd Avenue SE, turn left at Redmond Fall City Road SE, slight right at NE Tolt Hill Road, turn left at Fall City Carnation Road NE/Tolt Avenue, turn right at 334th Avenue NE, slight right at NE 42nd Street.

CARNATION CEMETERY

State Route 203, (North of) Carnation, WA 98014

A trading post built by a deserter of the Union Army was the first settlement for the town of Tolt. Quickly becoming a farming and logging community, the town prospered in spite of its remote location. In 1910, Elbridge Amos Stuart came to the area and started the Carnation Dairy Farm. Encompassing 750 acres, the farm became world famous as the "Home for Contended Cows." One cow produced more than 37,000 pounds of milk in one year. She even had famous visitors, including boxer Jack Dempsey.

In 1917, the town changed its name to Carnation, but many of the Indians and first settlers complained and it was changed back to Tolt in 1928. Finally, in 1951, the city changed its name back to Carnation and this time it stuck. But even today, you can still find people calling the town Tolt.

The Carnation cemetery was officially founded in 1905, and is the resting place for many of the loggers, farmers, and settlers of the area.

Are they coming back to dispute the name change? As you walk among the gravestones, you may hear footsteps following you around. Many people have seen a woman and her young son walking around the cemetery looking at the grave markers. There are reports of seeing black shapes and clouds dart about and hearing whispers and voices.

Visitors to the Carnation Cemetery hear footsteps following them around.

Most disturbing of all, is feeling stabbing pains and light-headedness when you are on the cemetery grounds.

 # SIGHTINGS: MONSTER OF LAKE WASHINGTON

Reports of people seeing and taking photographs of something coming up and eating ducks on Lake Washington have abounded since Seattle was founded. No one knows for sure what it is. It was once suggested that sturgeons were responsible, which may not be true. Reports of an eleven-foot long sturgeon found floating near Bellevue, sometime in the mid 1980s, claim these large sturgeons may have lived since the turn of the century. And who knows how many are still alive that may be even larger?

Sturgeon are bottom feeders and no matter how big they get, they just were not made to eat a squirming duck—their tastes tend to go more for snails and smaller fish.

Something is still lurking in the depths of Lake Washington waiting for its next meal—maybe waiting for you.

Directions from Carnation Cemetery to Central Tavern: Northwest on NE 42nd Street becomes 334th Avenue NE, turn left at Tolt River Road, continue on East Entwistle Street, turn left at Tolt Avenue, turn right at NE 32nd Street, turn right and stay on NE Tolt Hill Road, slight right at NE Redmond Fall City Road, continue on NE 85th Street, turn left at 3rd Street, turn right at Kirkland Avenue.

THE CENTRAL TAVERN

124 Kirkland Avenue, Kirkland, WA 98003

In 1936, two friends opened the Central Tavern across the street from its current location. Within a few years, the tavern was so successful, it relocated to its present home—a 1924 brick building.

Some employees and regular patrons have witnessed the "pink lady" appear in the rear of the building, either after closing or on slow nights when not many people are around.

The first Safeway grocery store in Kirkland was housed in the building before moving down the street in 1940 to a larger building.

Directions from the Central Tavern to Chateau Ste. Michelle Winery: East on Kirkland Avenue toward Main Street, turn left at 3rd Street, turn right at Central Way, take I-405 N to Everett, exit 20B for NE 124th Street, turn right at NE 124th Street, slight left at 132nd Avenue NE, turn right at NE 143rd Place, continue on 137th Place NE, continue on NE 145th Street, continue straight onto NE 145th Street.

CHATEAU STE. MICHELLE WINERY

14111 NE 145th Street, Woodinville, WA 98072
(425) 415-3633 △ www.ste-michelle.com
Open 10am - 5pm daily
Offers tours, cooking classes
check Web site for events, times, and prices

The Manor house was once owned by Seattle lumber and dairy tycoon Frederick Stimson. Stories say that Mr. Stimson was having an affair with a servant, and after learning of her pregnancy, the servant "accidentally" tripped on the stairs and tumbled to her death. When she isn't moving things, playing with the lights, or flushing toilets, you can find her roaming the hallways.

Mr. Stimson was the manager of the Stimson Lumber Company Mill in Ballard. He built a grand house on Queen Anne Hill for his family, but it just did not fit with their lives. So, in 1910, he purchased several hundred acres for a dairy farm in Woodinville. He named the dairy Hollywood after his wife and the hundreds of holly trees he planted. The dairy was state-of-the-art with its own power plant, and he soon started raising Holstein cattle ultimately improving the breed.

In 1921, while dressing at his home on Queen Anne Hill for a Thanksgiving dinner at Hollywood, he suffered a heart attack and died.

Bought in 1934, Chateau Ste. Michelle Winery is Washington States oldest winery.

Directions from Chateau Ste. Michelle Winery to Woodinville Cemetery: East on NE 145th Street, turn left at 148th Avenue NE, slight left at 140th Place NE.

WOODINVILLE CEMETERY

NE 175th Street, Woodinville, WA 98072

In 1898, two acres were given to the city of Woodinville for a cemetery from Ira and Susin Woodin, who settled in the area in 1871. A little over ten years later, and after a devastating diphtheria epidemic which took many lives including whole families, the Woodin's gave additional land to the cemetery. Records were not kept of the burials until the early 1900s; even then, they weren't the most accurate, but after a fire destroyed the records that *were* kept, the caretaker jotted down what he could remember on the back of a window shade.

No one knows for sure how many settlers were lost over time due to the fire, that destroyed the records. Spirits have been seen walking between the headstones and monuments of the cemetery. Many people have seen an apparition of a woman by the fence on the left side of the cemetery.

Directions from Woodinville Cemetery to the Oxford Saloon and Eatery: Head north on 140th Avenue NE toward NE 178th Street, slight right at Woodinville Snohomish Road NE, turn right at 108th Street SE/Marsh Road, turn left at Airport Way, turn right at 1st Street.

THE OXFORD SALOON AND EATERY

913 1st Street, Snohomish, WA 98290
(360) 568-3845
Sunday through Thursday 11am - 12 Midnight
Friday and Saturday 11am - 2am

The saloon once housed a brothel on the second floor and many of the working girls still remain in the building. The brothel's madam looks after her girls and the men who frequent the establishment.

Henry, a police officer, was stabbed to death during a bar fight at the saloon; you can see a photograph of him hanging by the stairs. Henry now likes to hang out in the women's restroom in the bar, frightening patrons as they freshen up.

Finally, one of the former owners throws items from the counter tops and likes to surprise women by pinching their derrières.

Directions from the Oxford Saloon and Eatery to Cabbage Patch Restaurant & Cattering: Head west on 1st Street toward Avenue A, turn right at Avenue A.

A former owner of the Oxford Saloon & Eatery surprises women with a pinch.

CABBAGE PATCH RESTAURANT & CATERING

111 Avenue A, Snohomish, WA 98290
(360) 568-9091 △ www.cabbagepatchrestaurant.com
Monday through Friday 10am - 10pm
Saturday and Sunday 8am - 10pm

The Cabbage Patch Restaurant occupies a house that was built in 1905. The building has also contained a boarding house and antique store.

Patrons and staff have reported dishes and other objects moving or falling to the ground, subsequently breaking. Others have reported of hearing dishes and glasses clinking in one of the upstairs dining rooms when no one is present. An apparition of a young girl has been seen looking out of the windows or just wandering the rooms of the restaurant.

In 1930, a young girl, Sybil Sibley, fell down a set of stairs and broke her neck. After following her family to this home in 1954, she never left.

Some patrons get the sensation of something brushing against them. This is said to be Sybil's dog.

Directions from the Cabbage Patch Restaurant to Snohomish Library: Head north on Avenue A toward 2nd Street, turn right at 2nd Street, turn left at Maple Avenue.

Workers and patrons to the Cabbage Patch Restaurant report dishes breaking with no one around.

SNOHOMISH LIBRARY

311 Maple Avenue, Snohomish, WA 98290
(360) 568-2898

November 12, 1894, the women of the Everett Book Club decided the town needed a library. They petitioned the mayor and started collecting books; two years later, they had about 1,000 books. With no official library yet, a temporary one was set up in a private home until a grant paid for the large Carnegie Library in 1905. In 2004, the library had outgrown its home at 105 Cedar Avenue and was moved with some of the original interiors to its current location on Maple Avenue.

Miss McMurchy was the librarian from 1923-1939, and she was well loved by all. Many patrons of the library have childhood memories of her teaching them to read or helping them find books. Miss McMurchy was a devout Presbyterian and would not put up with ghost stories or, in the very least, a haunted library, but it seems she changed her mind after she passed away. Having no estate when she passed, she was buried with no marker.

Some say that is why she hung around the library for so long. Many employees swear they have heard, seen or been touched by the frail librarian. She has been seen most often in the historic Carnegie area and especially near the children's story area. Some describe her as a small gray-haired woman wearing a blue dress. When it was discovered she did not have a grave marker, the cemetery donated a marble stone, and donations were raised for the engraving.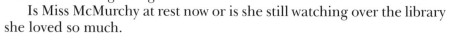

Is Miss McMurchy at rest now or is she still watching over the library she loved so much.

Directions from the Snohomish Library to the Bush House Hotel: South on Maple Avenue toward 3rd Street, turn left at 2nd Street, continue on 92nd Street SE, continue on 88th Street SE, turn right to merge onto WA-2, continue on West Stevens Avenue, turn left at Index-Galena Road, turn left at 5th Street.

The Bush House Hotel

300 Fifth Street, Index, WA 98256

People claim to see the apparition of a woman named "Alice" or, as some believe, Annabel. Alice and her husband were staying in room nine of the hotel, and one day, Alice received word that her husband had died in a mining accident where he worked. This was not true, but it was too late for Alice. Her husband came home to find her hanging dead in her room.

Rumors say the hotel was built over some graves, maybe even an old cemetery. A young girl is said to have drowned in the back of the hotel in one of the ponds, which have been since filled in. Another story is that someone fell, or jumped, off the third-floor terrace in the rear of the hotel to their death.

Index was a booming mining town in the 1880s. The hotel was built to provide housing and food for the miners and their families, as well as the workers who were constructing the Great Northern Railway. Index's population was minimal until in 1897, when the New Cooper veins were opened and operated by the Sunset Cooper Company. Then, sometime in 1889, the original hotel burned to the ground and was rebuilt.

A cleaning lady had an experience where someone named Annabelle spoke to her while she was cleaning a room; thinking a guest was in the bathroom, she did not think anything of it until, upon investigation, no one was found. Some employees get an odd feeling and will not go

The Bush House Hotel is where the apparition of 'Alice' has been seen.

upstairs by themselves. Even though lavender is found all over the outside of the hotel, it is smelled in the hallways and in some rooms in the dead of winter. Doors move on their own and a woman has been seen looking out some of the windows on different occasions and moving about the hotel. A resident of the cottage house claimed to see the curtains part as if someone was looking out, and sometimes saw a blue flicker of a television turning on and off in the upstairs windows. She claims the lights turn on and off and that you can hear the sounds of doors opening and closing, but upon inspection, the doors are in the same place as before, and appear never to have been moved.

The Bush House Hotel has a cottage next door, which used to be housing for the owners, a woman, and her three children who have been seen looking out of the cottage window.

Most of the claims sound as if they are just the normal goings on of the hotel, but in the past few years, work on the hotel was stopped abruptly and the building has started to crumble. The cottage house next door is a private residence and the hotel was recently purchased. It is not known what will happen to this building but please obtain proper permission before you trespass.

Directions from the Bush House Hotel to Skykomish Hotel: Return to WA-2, turn left, continue to Sky River Lane, and turn right.

Skykomish Hotel

5th Street North & Railroad Avenue - Skykomish, WA 98288

Skykomish was a railroad town built for fueling the Great Northern Railway trains on their way through the Cascade Mountains. At its peak, the town housed several thousand people. Although the town is still a base for railroad maintenance crews, it is a mere ghost town compared to the past. Unfortunately, careless waste disposal practices have resulted in soil and groundwater contamination in the area. Massive excavations of the ground have started taking place in 2006, and will continue for many years after. As a result, many of the historic buildings and houses in the town will have to be relocated.

Skykomish Hotel once housed a brothel, and one of the previous owners claims to have encountered Mary, a prostitute from the 1920s

Workers at the Skykomish Hotel claim lights turn on and off by themselves.

who was murdered by one of her customers in room thirty-two and has been at the hotel ever since. Workers in the hotel have reported seeing a woman in a white negligee standing quietly in the shadows. On other occasions, she has been known to follow workers around and turn on and off lights and open locked doors.

The first floor used to house a restaurant and employees have heard the sound of silverware clinking in the dinning room, even before any of the guests arrive for the breakfast rush.

Directions from Skykomish Hotel to Wellington: Return to WA-2, turn right and follow road up to Stevens Pass, the town of Wellington is on your left at the pass.

WELLINGTON

Stevens Pass, WA

The town of Wellington became famous in the United States for the worst avalanche disaster during the early 1900s. On March 1, 1910, two Great Northern Railway trains were stalled in the town of Wellington waiting for the track to clear; one was a passenger train while the other was a mail train. The snowplows were out of coal and the snow was falling a foot an hour with an electrical storm raging as well. In the middle of the night, the avalanche hit, sweeping both trains down the mountain into the Tye River Valley. The force of the avalanche, coupled with boulders and trees, left the trains as twisted metal on the valley floor. Ninety-six people died, but the number is still in dispute—the newspapers reported 118 fatalities. Some say the railroads persuaded officials to lower the death count; in fact, some bodies were never recovered.

After the tragic event, the town changed its name to Tye, trying to distance itself from the tragedy. Soon after, a new train tunnel was built and the town of Wellington was abandoned. There are two buildings left that were in place at the time of the disaster, but the train depot burned down in 1930. The town is now being dug up to control contamination from the past railroad waste. Several artifacts have been discovered, and if human remains are found, all clean-up work will stop.

Reports claim you can still see some of the train cars in the valley below. If you are hiking down the trail to the town, you may catch some of screams from the passengers on that fateful day. Reports of hearing phantom trains are also common.

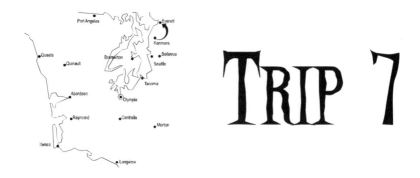

TRIP 7

KENMORE TO EVERETT

Beginning Directions: From Interstate 405 exit 20A for NE 116th Street, turn left at NE 116th Street, NE 116th Street turns into Juanita Drive NE.

SAINT EDWARD STATE PARK

14445 Juanita Drive NE, Kenmore, WA 98028

Once a Catholic seminary, Saint Edward State Park has 3,000 feet of shoreline and encompasses 316 acres. The land is also home to Bastyr University.

Visitors to the park claim of hearing and seeing ghostly children playing in and around the playground. Inside the old Seminary, light fixtures sway and are occasionally turned on by an unseen hand. The basement is a hotbed of activity—chairs and chalkboards are among items which are rearranged daily.

In 1931, Edward Seminary was constructed and, in 1958, the new Saint Thomas Seminary was finally finished, becoming a school for theology and collegiate students. After declining enrollment, the seminary was closed in 1977. The diocese sold the land to the State of Washington and the seminary building was then leased to Bastyr University.

Directions from Edward Seminary to Edmonds Theater: Northwest on Juanita Street NE, continue on 68th Avenue NE, turn left at NE Brothell Way, turn right at Ballinger Way NE, continue on Sunset Avenue, turn right at Main Street.

76

EDMONDS THEATER

415 Main Street, Edmonds, WA 98020
(425) 778-4554 △ www.edmondstheater.com

Built in 1923, the theater was always a family-run affair; even after restoration took place, a private owner still takes care of the place. People have seen a glowing figure of a man floating down the aisle of the theater.

Directions from Edmonds Theater to Frances Anderson Leisure and Cultural Arts Center: Head Southeast on Main Street toward 5th Avenue North.

FRANCES ANDERSON LEISURE AND CULTURAL ARTS CENTER

700 Main Street, Edmonds, WA 98020

The Edmonds Grade School was built in 1891 and was the first official schoolhouse; previously school was held in a barn owned by the town's founder. The school was a grand three-story Victorian building, but in 1928, a new building replaced that structure and after declining enrollment the school was closed in 1972.

A long-time teacher and principal, Francis Anderson, still watches over the schoolhouse tending to the ghostly students she loved so much; she is seen silently floating in the hallways. Reports that the children still hang around are abundant and young screams and laughing can be heard in the schoolhouse as well as children running in the hallways.

SIGHTINGS: MARINER HIGH SCHOOL

Edmonds, WA 98020

Around midnight, the hallway lights are suppose to be on at the Mariner High School. But occasionally, the lights are off and if you are close enough to the school, and you look hard enough, you can see glowing eyes looking out from one of the windows. Sources say that if the light is just right, you can see the body of a winged man.

Directions from Frances Anderson Leisure and Cultural Arts Center to Mallard Cove Apartments: East on Main Street toward 8th Avenue North, turn left at 9th Avenue North, turn right at 9th Avenue, turn left at WA-99, turn right at Airport Road, turn left at Admiralty Way.

MALLARD COVE APARTMENTS

12402 Admiralty Way, Everett, WA 98204
(425) 353-1100

Bill Stein, a taxi cab driver died as a result of a heart attack one night at the Mallard Cove Apartments while dropping off a passenger. He now haunts the apartment building and its residents. He is known to pick up the phone and will write down real addresses, perhaps for the next passenger in his taxi. In the morning, residents find his mysterious notes by the telephone and the door open. Some residents have seen his spirit and describe him as a man in his late forties, wearing a Mariner ball cap, sweats, and a t-shirt. Bill died in 1999.

Directions from the Mallard Cove Apartments to Everett Inn: Southwest on Admiralty Way, turn left on Airport Road, continue on 128th Street SW, turn left at 4th Avenue West.

EVERETT INN

12619 4th Avenue West, Everett, WA 98204

After the cleaning staff leaves for the night, the spirits take over the chores. A man dressed in dark janitor coveralls has been seen walking in the hallway, apparently keeping up the duties he once preformed long ago at the Inn. The sound of the washer and dryer doors opening and slamming shut are often heard; when checked, nothing appears to have been moved. A security camera was installed in the basement where most of the activity takes place, and on separate occasions, a mist has been seen in the camera. Afterwards, many loud banging noises are heard.

One guest's young daughter somehow would coax the elevator into going down into the basement, bypassing the key lock that had been put in place to limit guests from entering the basement. On one trip down to the basement, she was heard holding conversation with someone, but no one was in the basement at the time. Sometimes you could faintly hear a mumbling voice but it was unclear what was being said. Upon retrieving the young girl out of the basement, no one was seen, and the employee felt very uneasy in that space.

Some think the spirit is an elderly man who was a past employee of the hotel returning to continue his job.

Directions from the Everett Inn to Rucker Mansion: South on 4th Avenue West, turn left at 128th Street SW, turn left onto I-5 N, exit 41st Street SE, turn left at 41st Street SE, turn right at Rucker Avenue, turn left at 33rd Street, turn left at Laurel Drive.

RUCKER MANSION

412 Laurel Avenue, Everett, WA 98201

The Rucker Mansion, which sits quietly on top of Rucker Hill, was built in 1905 as a wedding present to Bethel Rucker's new wife, Ruby Brown. After a honeymoon in Asia, the couple returned to the mansion. Already occupying the large house was Ruby's mother-in-law, Jane, and her brother-in-law, Wyatt. The house was so large, I'm sure it was not a problem. It was decorated with the finest wood and even boasted having the state's first elevator.

Piano music is heard billowing from the Rucker Mansion when no one is home.

The Ruckers were among the city's founding families and owned the local railway. Unfortunately, two years after moving in, Jane Rucker died in the house of natural causes at the age of seventy-seven. The Ruckers ended up selling the home in 1923 to Clyde Walton for $32,500, considerably less than it was built for some eighteen years earlier. Walton lived in the home until his death in 1959.

It is currently a private residence but is opened occasionally to historical tours and special teas.

Music can be heard throughout the house when no one is home. Is this a memory from a long-ago party or Jane playing the piano?

In 2008, vandals destroyed many tombstones in the Evergreen Cemetery where the Rucker family has a huge pyramid mausoleum, which cost $30,000 to build. Twenty-two crypts are in the structure with only about half filled with family members. The vandals tried to break in to the mausoleum and even carved in the granite door.

Directions from Rucker Mansion to Everett High School: Northeast on Laurel Drive, slight right at 34th Street, turn left at Kromer Avenue, turn left at Bond Street, turn right at Terminal Avenue, continue on Everett Avenue, turn left at Colby Avenue.

EVERETT HIGH SCHOOL

2416 Colby Avenue - Everett, WA 98201

Some locals claim the school is haunted. Rumors persist that a spirit of a man has been seen wandering the school grounds and sometimes in the school itself. When the school was being built a construction worker fell to his death.

Does a construction worker haunt the Everett High School?

Directions from Everett High School to the *Equator* Schooner: Head south on Colby Avenue, turn right at 25ᵗʰ Street, turn right at West Marine Drive, turn left at 10ᵗʰ Street boat dock (where Marine Park and boat launch sign takes you).

THE EQUATOR SCHOONER

Boat Dock, Everett, WA 98201
www.portofeverett.com

The *Equator* once carried Robert Louis Stevenson, author of the classic book *Treasure Island*, and his family, including his friend, King Kalakaua of Hawaii. The renowned Matthew Turner built the schooner in 1888 and it served its first years on the South Seas as a copra trader and mail ship. Stevenson sailed on the schooner in 1889 and in 1890, which inspired him to write the story, "The Wrecker" in the book *Tales of the South Seas,* as well as being referenced in various works he penned.

At the turn of the century, the steam was installed in the schooner and it served as tender to an artic whaling fleet; by 1915, it had turned into a towing vessel and later was converted to diesel. In 1923, the *Equator* got stranded on the Quilleute River Bar and filled with water. She was refloated and towed back to Seattle. Fixed up again, she served many more years for

the Puget Sound Tug and Barge Company. Finally, in 1953, her machinery was torn out and she was abandoned. In the past, many people have tried to restore her but the schooner seems to be content to stay on dry land. In 1972, the worn schooner was put on the National Register for Historic Places.

It seems that the 1880s schooner is still carrying its passengers from long ago. A séance revealed that Stevenson and his pal, King Kalakaua, are still sailing the South Seas, playing poker and singing songs. Long dead sailors are also seen as balls of lights floating above the rotted deck.

Mysterious balls of light are seen hovering above the Equator Schooner.

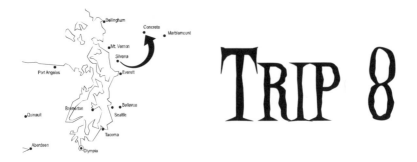

TRIP 8

SILVANA TO CONCRETE

Beginning Directions: From Interstate 5 exit Pioneer Highway East, head West to Larson Road.

LITTLE WHITE CHURCH

1717 Larson Road, Silvana, WA 98287
(360) 652-8739
Services July & August at 10am

Thirteen families met in 1894 to organize a second Lutheran church for the village of Silvana. Upset that the current Zion Lutheran Church mainly held services in their native Norwegian language, they formed the Salem Lutheran Church. The first services were held in 1890, and after many years, divided in 1963; the two churches allied and became the Peace Lutheran Church. The last full service in the Salem Church was in 1978, as both churches' congregations moved into a new building. After many years of neglect, the Salem Lutheran Church was restored to its former glory and renamed Little White Church on the Hill.

Now the dramatic building holds services two months in the summer and on Christmas Eve. The church also opens for weddings and other special occasions.

Some say that a young woman fell to her death from the steeple of the church and others swear she was murdered—but either story has the same haunting. At night, you can hear her screams and her ghost has

A spirit of a young woman has been seen floating near the Little White Church.

been seen in the church or wandering the grounds nearby. The cemetery is located just adjacent to the church and the rumor is that many strange sounds emit from the area, as well as always feeling like you are being followed, even in broad daylight.

Directions from Little White Church to the Trestle Bridge: Off Pioneer Highway, take first left after Little White Church just after leaving Silvana.

TRESTLE BRIDGE

Silvana, WA 98287

Many years ago a boy hung himself from the trestle bridge after his prom date left him for another. The body was discovered as a car went around the corner and struck it as the strangled boy dangled from the bridge.

The boy's footsteps are heard walking under the bridge late at night. Reports of cars stalling, failing to start, and other mechanical problems near the bridge are common.

Don't turn off your vehicle near the Trestle Bridge, it may not start again.

 # SIGHTINGS: FIRETRAIL

Marysville to Stanwood, WA

Motorists report seeing a man running next to their vehicles, peering in through the windows. He keeps up, going at speeds of thirty-five to forty miles-per-hour, even up a steep hill. Indians have been reported standing on the side of the road, then disappearing when a second look is taken. An uninvited passenger may take up your backseat only to be seen in your rear view mirror. If you turn around he will disappear. Lighted lanterns carried by ghostly shadows have been seen crossing the road at different intersections.

Legends state that Firetrail got its name when fire engulfed the backwoods of the area and quickly rushed down the road killing many. Others claim that the Indians used this trail to access their land. The Indians were later driven from this land.

Directions from the Trestle Bridge to Pioneer Cemetery: Return back to Pioneer Highway, turn left at 268th Street NE, turn right at 104th Avenue.

PIONEER CEMETERY

23800 104th Avenue, Stanwood, WA 98292

A large black haunting shadow has been seen near the big memorial headstone. Many people see swaying lanterns glowing in the night held by the hands of spirits around the neighborhood and in the cemetery. When approached the lanterns will fade into the dark of the night.

Directions from Pioneer Cemetery to Stanwood Museum & Pearson House Museum: Head north on 104th Avenue, turn right at 272nd Place NW.

STANWOOD MUSEUM & PEARSON HOUSE MUSEUM

102nd Avenue NW, Stanwood, WA 98292

The Pearson House was built in 1890, and served as the home of the first mayor of Stanwood. The former owners still watch over their home, especially now since it has become a museum.

After the house is locked up at night, candlelight glows in the windows and curtains move throughout the house.

Directions from Stanwood Museum & Pearson House Museum to Milltown & Milltown Cemetery: North on 102nd Avenue NW, continue on Old Pacific Highway, turn left at Pioneer Highway, go down the gravel road about ½ mile to the dead end.

MILLTOWN & MILLTOWN CEMETERY

Milltown, WA 98238

The town is overgrown and a few rotted cabins still exist. Milltown Cemetery is on the left over the train tracks; go right up the hill about one half mile.

Strange occurrences are common in this area, lights will appear and seem to come towards you, then disappear.

Directions from Milltown & Milltown Cemetery to Northern State Hospital: Head east on Milltown Road, turn left to merge onto I-5 N, take exit 230 for WA-

A Milltown Building. Strange lights are seen in Milltown.

20 toward Anacortes/Burlington, turn right at West Rio Vista Avenue, turn left at South Burlington Boulevard, turn right at East Fairhaven Avenue, turn right at Moiser Road, turn left at Fruitdale Road, turn right at Northwood Lane.

NORTHERN STATE HOSPITAL

7782 Northern State Road, Sedro Wooley, WA 98284

Northern State Hospital in Sedro Wooley was commissioned in 1909 and the first building opened in 1910. Bughouse is what the locals called it, and, in fact, it was a common term for an asylum as it is found in the Webster's dictionary of 1913. Northern State hospital was a large self-sufficient compound and used its patients to run the facilities. The patients were taught all kinds of trades, from farming to machine shop work. Many of its patients weren't mentally ill, as we would define it today. Some were even women whose husbands called them hysterical after entering menopause. Many of these men were just manipulating the system. Who knows the real reason why some of these patients were committed?

Will you encounter the spirit of a nurse at the Northern State Hospital?

Eventually, the hospital grew into one of the most respected facilities in the country. In 1976, the hospital closed and slowly has fallen into disrepair.

Some of the buildings from the Northern State Hospital currently house the Cascade Job Corps. Many of the students report activity from their dorm rooms. Rumors of tunnels and bunkers under the hospital are all possibly true.

The cemetery fell into disrepair as well and now hundreds of graves are unmarked.

There are many stories surrounding this hospital and the job corps. Reports are of apparitions, lights, shadows moving, cold spots, and strange noises. Several famous stories involve a little girl bouncing a red ball and a nurse who committed suicide. Visitors who have taken photographs get unusual anomalies and even human faces and people in their pictures. Voices are heard in the nurses' dorms as well as objects flying off shelves and moving around by themselves.

Directions from the Northern State Hospital to Concrete: Head south on Old Northern State Hospital Road, continue on North Sound Drive, turn right at Thompson Drive, slight left at Fruitdale Road, turn left at WA-20.

CONCRETE

Concrete, WA 98237

In 1858, prospectors started coming to the area of Concrete looking for gold. Instead, some found an area rich in limestone and clay, which is the basis for the material of concrete.

The Portland Cement Company set up shop around 1905 and "concrete city" sprang up around the factory. Later, another cement plant came into town and started up on the other side of town. After two devastating fires that destroyed most of the town, an ordinance was passed in 1921 regulating the rebuilding of the town to be fireproof. The town was rebuilt from the local cement, and after World War II, the preferred building type in concrete was concrete block.

Reports of ghostly going-ons in most of the main street buildings are part of the daily life in the small town of Concrete.

THE HUB TAVERN

45914 Main Street, Concrete, WA 98237

Spirits can be seen all over the small town of Concrete.

In the Hub Tavern, where more than just apparitions are seen of a grungy miner, objects move by themselves, lights turn on and off, and chairs have been known to rearrange themselves.

THE CONCRETE THEATER

45930 Main Street, Concrete, WA 98237
(360) 853-8458 △ **www.concretetheatre.net**

Built in 1923, the Concrete Theater hosted everything from boxing matches to vaudeville; after closing and falling into disrepear it has since been reopened and hosts concerts, movies, and can be rented for private events.

Psychics claim a young girl was murdered and her body was hidden in the basement of the theater. She remains there not realizing that she has died; her murderer remains at the theater as well tormenting paranormal investigators. The little girl mainly hangs out in the ladies' restroom. Finally, the last presence at the theater is thought to be the previous owner—when he is around, you can smell cigar smoke.

MOUNT BAKER HOTEL

45951 Main Street, Concrete, WA 98237
(360) 853-7922

Built in 1924, the first floor of the historic Mount Baker Hotel is the location of Cottage Café. Silverware has been known to move, doors open on their own, voices are heard, and several cold spots are also reported. A young man who was killed during the Vietnam War hangs around waiting for his girlfriend to show up. An apparition of a woman in 1940s attire has been seen near the antique phonograph.

Other haunted locations in Concrete include the Cajun Bar and Grill, Baker River Trading Post, Cascade Supply, Versatile Dreams, and the Summit Bank.

89

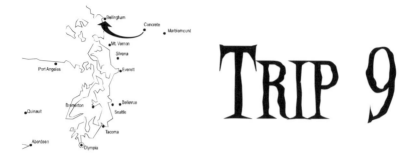

TRIP 9

BELLINGHAM

Beginning Directions: From Interstate 5 exit Old Fairhaven Parkway, head West to 12th Street, turn right.

FAIRHAVEN

Bellingham, WA 98225

On December 21st each year, a phantom freight train is heard barreling down ghostly tracks on its way to Skagit. On that date in 1892, a freight train pulled out of the station heading down through Happy Valley to unload its cargo in Skagit, stopping along the way at stations and to fuel up on coal and water. The trestle on the way had been compromised earlier by a freight carrying heavy logs, which had splintered some of the supports of the wooden trestle. The watchman had sent for a crew to fix the trestle, but that would take several hours and the superintendent insisted the train would be safe to cross without the needed repairs. As the freight train made its way across the trestle, the bridge gave way and the train plummeted to the valley and into the river below, killing the three men aboard.

Now, each year, the freight train barrels down tracks that have long been removed, stopping at each station, fuelling up and stopping for water along the way, until it reaches the trestle where it drops to the river below.

THREE FRENCH HENS

1100 Harris Avenue, Bellingham, WA 98225
(360) 756-1047 △ www.threefrenchhens.net
Monday through Saturday 10am - 6pm
Sunday 12pm - 5pm

The Nelson Block Bank Building was built in 1900 with a bank on the first floor. The second and third floors became offices. Today, a restaurant and a boutique reside on the ground level of the building.

Reports of hearing footsteps on the upper floors are common. A young woman died in a dentist chair during the 1950s and she is said to be the one walking around. But accounts are that it sounds like she is walking on glass and there is no reason (that is known) for this. She also makes appearances and is heard.

A man has also been heard coughing and clearing his throat in the building. Workers from the restaurant report lots of unexplained activity

The Nelson Block Bank Building. Almost all the buildings in Fairhaven have a ghost story attached.

from eerie noises to objects disappearing and reappearing later in a different unusual spot. The basement was the meeting hall for a secret society in the early 1900s. During renovations of the building in the 1970s, a human skeleton was found buried in the basement. The boutique, Three French Hens, currently occupies the bank part of the building.

PACIFIC CHEF

1210 Eleventh Street, Bellingham, WA 98225
(360) 676-1199 △ **www.pacificchef.com**

The Pythias Hall building was built in 1891 and housed two secret societies and many other businesses through the years. The building is named after the Secret Society of the Knights of Pythias. Founded in 1864 in Washington D.C., the mission of this fraternal order is to promote friendship among men and relieve suffering. This society is the first American Order ever chartered by an Act of Congress.

Pacific Chef is now resident of this building as well as the Colophon Café and several other shops.

Employees report the sounds of footsteps from above walking the rooms and hallways late at night. Customers have reported poltergeist activity in the Colophon Café, glasses and silverware are known to rearrange themselves and condiments on the tables have been known to move in sync when no one is looking. Incidents in the kitchen are common as well, freshly prepared meals come up missing or parts of the meal will mysteriously move to another part of the kitchen.

The basement of the building, located in the rear, was once a brothel. Access to the rear of the building renders a surprise as you stumble upon Fairhaven's own founder Dirty Dan Harris and the Village Green where summer movies are shown.

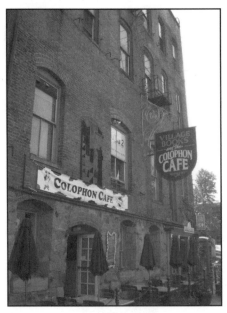
Ghostly footsteps can be heard in the Pythias Hall building.

SYCAMORE BLOCK

1200 Howard Avenue, Bellingham, WA 98225
(360) 733-6800 △ **www.sycamoresquare.com**

Sycamore Block was built during the economic boom in Fairhaven. The building housed professional offices including a gentleman's social club called the Cascade Club; such notable visitors to the club included Mark Twain and President William Howard Taft. The building is famous for the "Lady in Green" ghost. She was the wife of the town marshal, Joseph Blakely. Flora Blakely lived in an apartment on the fourth floor, and during childbirth in 1894, she passed away. Her wake and viewing was held in the lobby and was well attended by all the influential people of the time.

Cold spots are felt all over the building and on the fourth floor where the Cascade Club was located; the sounds of music and laughter can be heard.

On the other side of the fourth floor, where Flora's apartment may have been, reports reveal that the chairs in the businesses will be turned around to view Bellingham Bay during the evening. Other anomalies occur as well; the glass doors shake, and doors will not stay closed or will not open.

Directions from Sycamore Block to Fairhaven: Head North on 11th Street, slight left at Finnegan Way, continue on 11th Street, slight right at S State Street, turn right at Cedar Street, turn left at N Garden Street, turn right at E Pine Street.

THE WILSON LIBRARY

516 High Street, Bellingham, WA 98225
(360) 650-3050

Mabel Zoe Wilson helped create and make the first card catalog for the library in 1928. The six-story building has many stories of paranormal. In the microfilm room, cold spots and an occasional breeze has been reported, and the elevator at different times only wants to go to the third or fifth floor. Doors open and close, different weird smells are reported, and objects move on their own. Is this all the work of Ms. Wilson?

In 1964, the librarian fell down some stairs in her apartment building on Garden Street. Never recovering from her injuries, she died a few months later. Subsequently, the library was dedicated in her memory and she seems to have stuck around the building, keeping up her duties as well as going home to her apartment each night after work.

Directions from the Wilson Library to Bayview Cemetery: Head northwest on East Pine Street, turn right at North Garden Street, turn right at East Chestnut Street, turn left at Ellis Street, turn right at Lakeway Drive, turn at Woburn Street.

BAYVIEW CEMETERY

1420 Woburn Street, Bellingham, WA 98229

Founded in 1887, the first bodies were laid to rest in 1888 at the Bayview Cemetery. The cemetery encompasses a total of 234 acres, with only fifty acres being used currently. After a visit to the resting place of thousands with headstones of all types and ages covered in macabre looking moss and trees growing through some of the headstones, it's easy to tell why so many legends surround this cemetery. Some of the headstones are over a hundred years old, while others are new.

At one of the more famous monuments called "Angel Eyes," an apparition of a woman has been seen wandering nearby. Visitors claim this woman resides beneath the monument and no one knows for sure why she is not at rest.

Another nearby monument with a story is one of the many "Tables." This table is said to summon an early death if laid upon. I am not sure how many people have lain on this table to constitute this urban myth, but I'm not going to try it out.

An apparition has been seen wandering close to a stone wall and since there are many small walls in the cemetery, which one could not be pinpointed exactly. Other activity includes mysterious apparitions seen wandering the graves, lights floating, and strange unexplained mists billowing through the cemetery.

Directions from Bayview Cemetery to Mt. Baker Theatre: Southeast on Woburn Street, turn right at Lake Street, turn right at Ellis Street, turn left at Champion Street, turn right at North Commercial Street.

MT. BAKER THEATRE

104 North Commercial Street, Bellingham, WA 98225
(360) 734-6080 △ www.mountbakertheatre.com

The former owner of the Mt. Baker Theater still keeps tabs on how things are running.

The theatre opened on April 29, 1927, and since that day, occurrences have happened there, usually after patrons have left for the night. At night, when the theater is vacant, balls of light float through the air, the sounds of skirts rustle, and gusts of cold wind blow through the building.

The former owner of the property is still hanging around even after she was evicted from her house, so the theater could be built on that site. Three buildings all together were torn down to build the elaborate theater, a church, and two houses—one which was a brothel. When the theatre was built, there was no need for another one, since more than a dozen theaters in the little town already existed. Fox West Coast Theaters from California thought this town was right for a large vaudeville theater, and they were right. The Mt. Baker Theatre has never closed and continues to be successful, even with its spirits.

95

SIGHTINGS: NOOKSACK RIVER

Whatcom County, WA

During the salmon run in 1967, several fishermen on the Nooksack River saw Bigfoot. Tracks from thirteen and a half inches, with a forty-five inch stride were reported. Indians tell tales of hairy ghosts in the area.

Directions from Mt. Baker Theatre to Overland Block and Bellingham: Head south on North Commercial Street, turn right at West Champion Street, turn left at West Holly Street.

OVERLAND BLOCK AND BELLINGHAM

316 West Holly Street, Bellingham, WA 98225
(360) 671-4431
Monday through Saturday 7am - 3pm
Sunday 8am - 2am

Full of antique stores, restaurants, and novelty stores, the city of Bellingham was once four separate towns on Bellingham Bay; by 1903, they finally came together as one city. The four towns struggled as many ventures came and went.

Watcom was an 1858 gold rush town, and housed the lumber mill. At one time, there were more people living in the small inlet that lead up the Fraser River than in the entire territory of Washington, but after a better way to go up the river was found, the population dwindled back to a mere 100 people.

Sehome, a coal-mining town, was a bust after the coal ran out; Sehome is now Bellingham's downtown.

Unionville was another coal town, but these mines failed also. In 1888, the lots that the coal company had purchased for the workers' houses were bought by a developer and incorporated into Fairhaven.

Fairhaven was on its way to becoming the economic hub of the north sound; a developer had bought up the land and planned major businesses, a railroad, and steamships. Buildings went up so fast that alleys were forgotten. A housing boom and economic growth seemed promising, but after the depression of 1893, the town barely hung on.

The Overland block once housed a rooming house, bars, brothels, and gambling halls. The Overland block was built during the time of an economic boom in 1890. The building, which currently houses the Old Town Café, has had several different businesses within its walls: a clothing store, morgue, and the city hall. In the Old Town Café, witnesses have seen flatware and dishes move and fall for no reason, and music from a piano is heard by some of the regulars, playing a tune from the early 1900s. A woman also looks out from a second-story window. Was she a prostitute waiting for her "John" or just checking out the fashion of the day?

Directions from Overland Block and Bellingham to the Edward Eldridge Mansion: Northwest on Holly Street, continue on Eldridge Avenue.

The Mansion

2915 Eldridge Avenue, Bellingham, WA 98226

The Edward Eldridge Mansion you see now was built in 1926 and was the fourth house built on the site. A fire burned the first in 1878, the second in 1891, and the third in 1894. The fourth house had a fire as well in 1907, but only caused $7,000 worth of damage.

Edward Eldridge was one of the first settlers to Whatcom County. He started a lumber mill, but soon grew tired of this venture and tried his hand at mining. While mining, he became the first legislator ever elected from Whatcom County to the House of Territorial Legislature. Edward Eldridge died in 1898, and his family continued to prosper and live at the Eldridge Mansion until 1939.

During World War II, military officers occupied the house, and some people claim that a woman died in childbirth there, but no records of this exist. Her screams are still heard in the house. A young boy has been seen there as well as another unnamed spirit. Claims persist that objects move and voices are heard, and sometimes you can feel a tugging as if a child is trying to get your attention.

This house is a private residence.

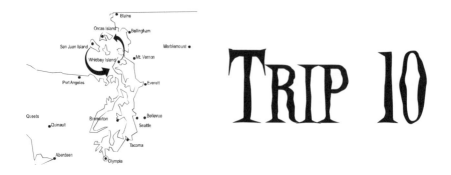

TRIP 10

ISLANDS

Beginning Directions: Islands are accessible by ferry.

ROCHE HARBOR RESORT

CEMETERY MAUSOLEUM, FRIDAY HARBOR

Roche Harbor, WA 98250, San Juan Islands
(800) 451-8910 △ (360) 378-2155 △ www.rocheharbor.com

Roche Harbor started as Roche Harbor Lime and Cement Company in 1886, founded by John McMillin. The hotel was built around the bunkhouse called Hotel de Haro for customers negotiating the purchase of lime. Cottages for the married workers were built in 1886, and some of the cottages still exist today. A general store, offices, and other facilities for the company town were built over the years.

The site of Westpoint was originally the site of a Japanese settlement. The company employed them as gardeners, waiters, and cooks. Many of the workers and their families are buried in the cemetery; weather and time have rotted away the wooden markers leaving most of the graves unmarked. McMillin wished to leave a memorial of his beliefs and family. The monument looks like a table with six chairs surrounded by columns, with one built broken to signify the unfinished state of mans' work once he has died. The table and chairs in the center of the columns are to represent the family table, and each seat is for a family member. Under each chair is a crypt where the ashes of the family members are buried.

Late at night, when the moon is full, some say you can see his family sitting at the table talking and laughing. Rumors also claim that, during a rainstorm, no rain will fall on the table.

FORT CASEY

Whidbey Island, WA 98278

Fort Casey was one of the three forts that made up the Triangle of Fire for the defense of Puget Sound in the 1890s; the other two forts were Fort Flagler and Fort Warden, home of the Admiralty Head Lighthouse built in 1858. Fort Casey was founded in 1897.

The Fort Casey ghosts include apparitions and shadowy figures. Strange noises are reported by visitors as well as scratching on walls.

SUNNYSIDE CEMETERY

Coupeville, WA 98239, Whidbey Island
www.sunnysidecemetery.org

Isaac Ebey, a pioneer of Whidbey Island, was tragically killed and scalped by the local Kake Indians. After many years, Isaac's "poor head" was finally recovered and returned to Isaac's brother, Winfield. Some say he immediately buried the scalp, but there is no mention of this in the immaculate diaries he kept.

When Winfield died, the scalp was passed down through the family members, and more than fifteen years later, reports of the scalp, which still retained its long flowing black hair, surfaced from a family member now living in San Francisco, California.

Residents of the island recount tales of seeing both a headless ghosts and an apparition with his head intact walking around in the Ebey part of the cemetery.

Some residents claim to have seen apparitions around the blockhouse as well. Built in 1853 as a cabin, the building was converted into a blockhouse to protect against the Indians in 1857. Prior to white settlement in this area, the local Indian tribes would sometimes bury their dead in the ground, but most often in canoes placed in the branches of trees.

Keep an eye out when you visit the site; this whole area was disturbed when the whites settled the area.

ONE ROOM SCHOOLHOUSE

908 NW Alexander Street, Coupeville, WA 98239, Whidbey Island
(360) 678-3310 △ www.shermanmuseum.org
The museum offers tours of the schoolhouse.

A young ghost girl, dressed in a pinafore, can be seen looking from the window of the schoolhouse, as well as the porch.

ROSARIO RESORT & SPA

1400 Rosario Road, Eastsound, WA 98245, Orcas Island
(800) 562-8820 △ www.rosarioresort.com

Believing he only had a few years left, shipbuilder and Seattle mayor Robert Moran built his retirement home in 1909. As it turned out, the doctors were wrong and he had more than a few years left; Moran died in 1926.

Donald Rheem of Rheem Manufacturing of San Francisco purchased the house as a vacation home. His wife was soon living there full time. Alice Rheem was said to have a drinking and fidelity problem. Donald thought the new house would remove Alice from her situation and things would improve, but every time he was out of town, she would go back to her old ways. She died in 1937.

Alice may have died but she never left. She is seen wearing a red negligee and heard performing her bedroom activities at night. There are reports she also rides her motorcycle through the mansion and some hear lavish parties when no one is having a party.

At this writing, the resort is currently being auctioned off; as for its fate, we will have to wait and see.

TRIP 11

PENINSULA

SIGHTINGS: PURDY BRIDGE

Highway 16 by Gig Harbor, WA

Late in the 1970s, a car on the bridge hit a child. Now, as you drive across, a ghostly boy may dart across the bridge...be careful!

Beginning Directions: From State Route 16 exit SE Burley Olalla Road, head East.

STARVATION HEIGHTS

Olalla/Port Orchard, WA 98359

Dr. Linda Burfield Hazzard and her husband Sam ran a sanitarium at the turn of the century. She said she could cure disease by fasting, and patients flocked to her for her therapy. Many of them died due to her treatment of starvation.

At first, Dr. Hazzard buried and marked their graves with trees, but after a while, she ran out of room and started to throw their bodies off the cliff behind the building or down the well. Before they starved to death, she had the patients sign new wills, leaving everything to her. If

101

they died before she could get them to sign everything over, she just forged their signatures.

The doctor is gone, but you can still walk the forest where her patients were cured of disease through starvation. The entire area is said to be haunted.

The house is a private residence.

Directions from Starvation Heights to Frank Choop Place: WA-3, slight right at WA-30, continue on North Callow Avenue, turn right at 6th Street, turn left at Chester Avenue.

FRANK CHOOP PLACE

704 Chester Avenue, Bremerton, WA 98337
www.lihi.org

The ghostly patients of Harrison Naval Hospital still hang out with the current residents of the Frank Choop Place Apartments. The hospital opened in 1912 and was the county's only general hospital. It went through

Frank Choop Place. The former patients of Harrison Naval Hospital still inhabit the halls of this current apartment building.

a half dozen names and served as a nursing home before renovations in 1976 turned it into fifty-six studio and one-bedroom apartments.

Residents of the apartments complain of ghostly children running through the halls and stairs, objects moving, doors that open and close and lights that turn on and off by themselves. Numerous residents and guests have witnessed many spirits in the building as well. The spirits are usually seen walking around in the apartments as patients or as nurses taking care of ghostly patients. The hospital's morgue was housed in the basement; many sounds are heard from that area.

Directions from Frank Choop Place to Port Gamble: Head South on Chester Avenue, turn right at 6th Street, continue on Kitsap Way, take ramp to WA-3 N.

PORT GAMBLE

Port Gamble, WA 98264
(360) 297-8074 △ www.portgamble.com
Visit the museum or visit the Web site for a walking tour of the town

Port Gamble is a privately-owned National Historic Landmark. Originally a company town founded in 1853, now the town is restored to its original grandeur. Many of its structures house shops and restaurants, and the town offers maps and walking tours. Many of the haunted structures are easily found just strolling the streets.

WALKER AMES HOUSE

Built in 1888-1889, the Walker Ames House has lights that are reported turning on and off when no light bulbs are in the fixtures. A ghost woman has been seen on the third floor and feelings of being followed throughout the property are some of the reports.

In the Old Hospital, whispering is heard, items moving, and strange odors emanate through the building.

Ghostly children are heard running at the Post Office in Port Gamble.

POST OFFICE

Children are heard laughing and running through the upstairs section of the Post Office. A presence at the top of the stairs reportedly watches you. Murmuring voices, shuffling of feet and whistling are all heard down the hallways on the main floor of the building. The basement is where the morgue for the town used to be housed.

THEATER

Shadows have been seen both in the projection booth and on the stage area of the town's theater.

DREW HOUSE

In the Drew House, electronics are known to turn on and off. Footsteps are heard walking around the rooms and a faint sound of someone breathing close to you is known to occur.

DAVE OLSON HOUSE

Apparitions go about their daily business as if nothing has changed in the Dave Olson House. A little ghost girl is seen in the upstairs window, tapping impatiently as if trying to get your attention. The lights in the house sway on their own accord and turn on and off by themselves.

OLD MILL SITE

The Old Mill Site has had its share of deaths from men being crushed to decapitation. A headless man has been seen wandering the area. Is he searching for his head?

THOMPSON HOUSE

The Thompson House is the oldest occupied house in Washington State. Footsteps are heard walking upstairs.

House 57 is known for its doors opening and closing, and sometimes, you get the feeling of being pushed down the stairs.

Footsteps of the long-dead owner are heard in the Thompson House.

OLD SERVICE STATION

In the Old Service Station, objects have been known to move on their own accord.

HOUSE 69

People who have slept in House 69 have woken up to heavy breathing near their bed.

BUENA VISTA CEMETERY

The Buena Vista Cemetery has many spirits that are seen strolling among the graves.

Directions from Port Gamble to Manresa Castle: Head north on Rainier Avenue/WA-104, turn right to stay on WA-104, turn right at WA-20, turn left at Sheridan Street.

MANRESA CASTLE

7th & Sheridan Streets - Port Townsend, WA 98368
(360) 385-5750 △ (800) 372-1281 △ www.manresacastle.com

Built in 1892 for Charles Eisenbeis, Port Townsend's first mayor and his family occupied the house until his death in 1902. It then became vacant until 1928 when Jesuits purchased it; now the building is a hotel and restaurant.

Legend says that a Jesuit priest hung himself in the castle's circular attic. There is no official record of the suicide, but you can hear weird sounds and smell strange odors. Singing can be heard from the bathroom in room 306. In other areas of the hotel, a clock that has not worked for years is heard chiming. Lights turn on and off and doors open and close.

Kate, whose portrait hangs in the lounge, is also said to have had a doomed fate while at the castle. After getting word that her lover died at sea, she jumped out of one of the tower windows to her death. Recently employees at the hotel have said the stories of Kate and the priest were made up to satisfy curiosity seekers. The truth is, the hotel is haunted

Does the spirit of a Jesuit Priest haunt the Manresa Castle?

and lots of activity has been reported, but no one knows for sure who haunts the building and why.

Directions from Manresa Castle to the Palace Hotel: Head south on Sheridan Street towards West Sims Way.

THE PALACE HOTEL

1004 Water Street, Port Townsend. WA 98368
(360) 385-0773 △ (800) 962-0741 △ www.palacehotelpt.com

The Palace Hotel occupies the second and third floors of a building, which once stood as a brothel. The girls' cribs are now suites with private baths. Each room is named for one of the girls who once lived and worked there.

Even after the 1930s raid on the brothel, the girls still like to hang around and do their work. Beds shake and moans are heard, and shadowy figures dart around the rooms and hallways.

Directions from the Palace Hotel to Ann Starrett Mansion: Northeast on WA-20, turn left at Quincy Street, slight left at Jefferson Street, turn right at Adams Street, turn right at Clay Street.

ANN STARRETT MANSION

744 Clay Street, Port Townsend, WA 98638
(800) 321-0644 △ www.starrettmansion.com

The Victorian mansion built in 1889 by George Starrett for his wife, Ann, features a rare eight-sided dome tower. George commissioned George Chapman from New York to paint a solar calendar on the dome and Ann's likeness is used for the four seasons and the four virtues. Red colored glass was installed in each of the small dormer windows, so when the sun shines on the first day of each season, a red beam of light is projected on the appropriate panel showing the correct time of year. The dome also features a freestanding staircase and the man who installed the staircase never revealed how it was built.

At the Ann Starrett Mansion, a redheaded woman has been seen wandering the halls.

A redheaded woman's head has been seen peering out of the dome's windows. The innkeeper and guests have all reported seeing the same redheaded woman ghost wandering the halls.

Directions from Ann Starrett Mansion to Holly Hill House: Southwest on Clay Street, turn right at Polk Street.

HOLLY HILL HOUSE

611 Polk Street, Port Townsend, WA 98368
(360) 385-5619 △ (800) 435-1454 △ www.hollyhillhouse.com

Built in 1872 by Colonel Robert Hill, the house is currently a five-bedroom Victorian bed and breakfast.

A ghostly woman likes to walk the halls and play the piano in the house. You can view her portrait at the top of the stairs.

Also there is a man's spirit who is seen wearing turn-of-the-century clothing, and sometimes smokes cigars in one of the upstairs rooms.

Directions from Holly Hill House to Fort Warden State Park: Northwest on Polk Street, turn right at Lawrence Street, turn left at Tyler Street, becomes F Street, turn right at Cherry Street, turn right at West Street, turn left at Fort Warden State Park.

FORT WARDEN STATE PARK

200 Battery Way, Port Townsend, WA 98368
(360) 344-4400 △ www.lighthousefriends.com

Built as part of the "Triangle of Fire," Fort Warden was used as an active Army base from 1902 until 1953. In the fall of 1904, the headquarters of the Defense Command of Puget Sound was moved from Fort Flagler to Fort Warden, and by the next year, the fort was considered complete and fully functional.

World War I saw the arrival of soldiers preparing to be shipped off to the European front. In 1957, the State of Washington purchased the 433 acres and turned the property into a juvenile detention center, and in 1973, the site was reopened to the public as a state park.

Today, the Fort is open to the public for exploration, events, and even vacations. You can wander through the barracks or visit the balloon hanger, which housed airships during World War I.

THE POINT WILSON LIGHTHOUSE

The Point Wilson lighthouse was built in 1879 and automated in 1976.

A glowing apparition has been seen at the Point Wilson Lighthouse.

As you wander the grounds near the lighthouse, you might bump into a glowing apparition wearing a long gown. She has also been seen in and around the light keepers' house. Footsteps are heard and unseen hands move items.

The light keepers' home was turned into a duplex and currently sits vacant.

The Guard House

In the Guard House, a depressed soldier thinking of suicide shot himself. Today, he can't seem to rest and manifests often to unsuspecting visitors.

Cemetery

Visitors to the fort often see strange mists and glowing lights late at night in the cemetery. The wooded area next to it has had some claims that the woods are the most active part of the fort, and there seems to be some sort of connection between the wooded area and the soldier from the Guard House.

Visitors to the Guard House may encounter the spirit of a soldier who took his own life a hundred years ago.

THE PARADE GROUNDS

The Parade Grounds appears to have a residual haunting from the men lining up for formation. Visitors have seen the ghostly troops preparing for inspection on many occasions.

THE DORMS

The Dorms also are a site of residual haunting. You may hear the men going about their daily business in them.

Directions from Fort Warden State Park to McAlmond House: South on Fort Warden State Park, turn right on West Street, turn left at Cherry Street, continue on Walker Street, turn right at Washington Street, slight right at Sims Way, slight right at US-101, take exit toward South Sequim Avenue, turn right at South Sequim Avenue, continue on East Anderson Road, right at Twin View Drive.

McAlmond House

Twin View Drive, Sequim, WA 98382

Captain Elijah H. McAlmond built the two-story house overlooking the bay in 1861, and ever since, rumors that the house was used to smuggle Chinese into the United States have persisted in the small community. What else may have the house been involved in through the years? Was it a portal for smugglers during prohibition?

The McAlmond house remained in the family until the mid 1900s. Former residents of the house have claimed having eerie experiences when young girls stay in the house. On one occasion, the house groaned and creaked all night long. In the morning, the owners found one of the guest bedroom doors completely blocked by furniture, which had been stacked up from the inside. With no possible exit to the room once the door was blocked, the incident still remains unexplained.

The McAlmond house stands on a bluff west of the Dungeness River on Twin View Drive.

Directions from McAlmond House to Lake Crescent: East on Twin View Drive, turn right at East Anderson Road, turn left at Lotzgesell Road, turn left at Fortman Road, slight left at Kitchen Dick Road, turn right at WA-101, follow US-101 until you come to Lake Crescent Lodge.

Lake Crescent

Lake Crescent, WA 98362
www.nationalparkreservations.com

An Indian legend refers to the part of the spirit that passes on as the good part of the soul. The part that stays behind is called Tsiyatko; it is evil and unbalanced. The Tsiyatko spirits are often at war with each other. At one such war, the "Old One" came down and told them to stop. After ignoring his command, the "Old One" flooded the basin where they fought and the area is now called Lake Crescent. In the mist you can still see the Tsiyatko spirits trying to move on, but stuck in the basin by the water.

In 1916, a lodge was built at which President Franklin D. Roosevelt once stayed. The lake also offers a type of trout that resembles a steelhead.

The Beardslee trout is landlocked and can be found only in Lake Crescent.

The lake also holds another creepy secret; in the 1940s, two fishermen happened upon a body floating in the lake. Her body had saponified like ivory soap, and she had apparently been in the lake for years. Most of her face and fingers were decayed, but the rest of her body, and even clothing, were well preserved.

Within a year, investigators had identified the woman and she turned out to be an unfortunate waitress at the Lake Crescent Tavern. After two failed marriages, she tried for lucky number three. This final husband was abusive, and one day, killed her and dumped her body in the lake. This was a smart move for him since many people had drowned in the lake and their bodies were never recovered—probably because the lake was so deep and cold.

But I guess she had enough spirit to come back to get her revenge on him by reappearing in the lake.

SIGHTINGS: OLYMPIA NATIONAL FOREST

Olympia National Forest, WA

Hikers in the Olympia National Forest who get lost can always find their way back by listening for bagpipes playing. If you follow the sound, it will send you to safety.

Rumors say a man in the area used to play the bagpipes and was killed in the 1980s. Is he helping lost hikers out of the woods?

Directions from Lake Crescent to Native American Burial Grounds: Return to Olympic National Forest Road; turn right at West Snider Road, slight right at WA-101, turn left at Jackson Heights Drive.

Native American Burial Ground

Queets, WA 98331

Over the years, several guests visiting the burial ground have reported hearing the low beat of something surrounding them resembling the beat of drums and a far off sound of Indians singing.

Directions from the native American Burial Ground to Lake Quinault Lodge: Return to US-101, slight left at Old State Highway 9, slight left at South Shore Road.

Lake Quinault Lodge

Quinault, WA 98575
(866) 875-8456 △ www.nationalparkreservations.com

Vacationers used to come to Lake Quinault and stay at the Log Hotel as early as the late 1880s. In 1924, a fire broke out in the kitchen and burned most of the Log Hotel. The owners took this opportunity to build a grand lodge, built on the site of the old hotel in only fifty-three days. The workers labored day and night to complete this extraordinary lodge, and when possible, they salvaged remnants of the Log Hotel, including parts of the attic.

There was only one fatality from the fire—a cleaning woman who was caught in the attic and could not escape the smoke and flames. You can still feel her when you go up there (it's a small conference room now) and in the kitchen she throws glasses and silverware.

TRIP 12

HOQUIAM TO OYSTERVILLE

Beginning Directions: State Route 101 turns into Riverside Avenue.

POLSON MUSEUM

**1611 Riverside Avenue, Hoquiam, WA 98550
(360) 533-5862 △ www.polsonmuseum.org
December 27 through March 31: Saturday & Sunday 12pm - 4pm
April 1 through December 23: Wednesday through Saturday, 11am - 4pm
Sunday 12pm - 4pm**

The mansion which houses the modern day Polson Museum was a wedding present from Arnold Polson's uncle in 1924. Arnold Polson and his new bride lived and raised a family in the twenty-six-room mansion until 1965 when the family moved to Seattle. Arnold Polson died a few years later, in 1968, and after years of neglect, his widow donated the mansion to the city of Hoquiam in 1976.

Visitors and museum staff have witnessed the ghost of a little girl in the nursery area; perhaps it was the imprint of the Polson's daughter happily playing in her room. A lady has been seen as well in and around the property. Is that the spirit of Mrs. Polson coming back to the home she loved so much?

Directions from Polson Museum to Billy's Bar and Grill: Start out Northwest on Riverside Avenue, follow signs for US-101, continue on Heron Street/US-101.

BILLY'S BAR AND GRILL

322 E Heron Street, Aberdeen, WA 98520
(360) 533-7144 △ **www.techline.com/banners/billys/**
Monday through Saturday 8am - 11pm
Sundays 8am - 9pm

Named after Billy Gohl, Billy's Bar and Grill was built in 1906, and the bar has a unique back bar and the second floor has a reputation of being used as a brothel in the past. This location may or may not have been where the famous serial killer worked as a bartender at the turn of the century. Billy Gohl was responsible for at least forty-one floaters who were pulled out of the harbor between 1909 and 1912.

After Billy's bartending days, he worked as an agent for the Sailor's Union Hall. The sailors would come in from ships to collect their mail and do their banking. After talking with the sailors about local family and valuables they might have, Billy would kill the man and send him through a trap door down a chute to the Wishkah River, which let out to Gray's Harbor.

Arrested in 1913, he spent the rest of his life in prison, dying in 1928. Is he still on the lookout for more victims? Reports at the bar are of mirrors spontaneously fogging up as well as lights and other electronics turning on and off. Or, maybe it's the spirits of the young ladies who lived and worked upstairs, no one knows for sure.

SCHOOL CROSSING AHEAD

Directions from Billy's Bar and Grill to Tokeland Hotel and Restaurant:
Northeast on East Heron Street/US-101, follow signs for US-101, continue on to WA-105, turn right at Tokeland Road, turn left to stay on Tokeland Road, continue on to Fisher Street, slight left at Kindred Avenue, left at Hotel Street.

TOKELAND HOTEL AND RESTAURANT

100 Hotel Road, Tokeland WA 98590
(360) 267-7006 △ www.tokelandhotel.com

This country inn offers eighteen rooms and a restaurant, including plenty of spirits. The original owner's son drowned while playing in the mud at the strand. When the tide came in, he got stuck and perished. History states that he is buried on the hotel grounds, but no graves have been unearthed. Unseen little feet like to jump on the beds, messing up the sheets.

When the present owners bought the hotel, it had been abandoned for several years. Even with a long gravel drive, none of the original lead glassed windows had been broken and the owner believes a spirit is protecting the hotel.

In the early days of the hotel, the area was a port for the Chinese slave trade. The building was a safe house for escaped slaves. Rumor has it that a slave, Charlie Chan, perished in a spot behind the fireplace while he waited to be sent home. One report has a burly fisherman claiming his plate of food moved on it own accord in the restaurant. Strange lights have been seen and unknown mists appear suddenly as well as a ghostly cat and all have been reported in the hotel and restaurant.

Directions from Tokeland Hotel and Restaurant to Hannan Playhouse:
South on Hotel Street, turn right at Kindred Avenue, slight right at Fisher Street, turn left toward WA-105, turn left at WA-105 slight right at US-101, turn left at Franklin Street, turn left at 8th Street.

HANNAN PLAYHOUSE

518 8th Street, Raymond, WA 98577
(360) 942-5477

A small theater, only seating seventy-four, the Hannan Playhouse is known for a ghostly cat and the owner who still comes back to check on how the theater is being managed. Patrons and actors have seen a black cat gliding across the stage. It would not be unusual, but no animals live in the theater and the cat seems to just disappear when people come close to it. A shadow of a man has been seen in the control room and other ghostly activities seem to happen in the theater when least expected.

Directions from Hannan Playhouse to Rod's Lamplighter Restaurant: South on 8th Street, turn right at Franklin Street, turn left at US-101, turn left at Pacific Way, turn right at 39th Place, turn left at L Street.

Rod's Lamplighter Restaurant

3807 L Street, Long Beach, WA 98644

Employees and patrons alike have reported many strange occurrences at Rod's Lamplighter Restaurant—pool balls are known to move while people are choosing which ball to hit next, lights and other electronic devices turn on and off or switch channels on their own.

Directions from Rod's Lamplighter Restaurant to the Old School House: South on L Street, turn left at 38th Place, turn left at Pacific Highway, turn right at 40th Street, turn left at Peninsula Road.

The Old School House

School Street & Sundridge Road, Oysterville, WA 98641

Oysterville Schoolhouse is the third and last schoolhouse in Oysterville. Built in 1905, it stands in place of the two previous schoolhouses.

Legend says that a child died from an epileptic seizure while at school one day. The child is occasionally spotted, as shadows dart about the building.

Stop by the church and pick up a walking tour. The schoolhouse is number 16 on the tour.

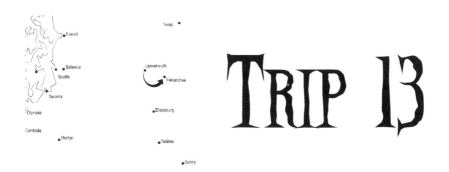

TRIP 13

LEAVENWORTH TO WENATCHEE

Beginning Directions: State Route 2..

LEAVENWORTH

Leavenworth was not always as it appears today. After the end of the railroad and timber era, Leavenworth fought back against dying into just another small town. In the 1960s, Leavenworth changed into the Bavarian town that it is now.

TUMWATER INN RESTAURANT

219 9th Street, Leavenworth, WA 98226
(509) 548-4232 △ www.tumwaterinn.com

The Tumwater Inn Restaurant is known for its century old piano and comfortable setting, and the restaurant has a few customers that have never left.

A little girl is said to be associated with the piano; she likes to move photographs and glasses in the bar area. An older man has been seen in the kitchen area; perhaps he is keeping watch on the staff.

EDELWEISS HOTEL

843 Front Street, Leavenworth, WA 98226
(509) 548-2220

The Edelweiss Hotel was built in 1901 and once housed a brothel, but now is a hotel on the main square of Leavenworth. The ground level of the hotel holds several different shops—Der Goldsmith, Ganz Klasse and Schocolat.

Reports of ghostly activity come from the hotel as well as the stores beneath. The building was the first to be changed to the Bavarian look and is in the center of town—and perhaps the center of ghostly activity. Reports of lights turning on and off as well as objects moving on their own have been reported by many of the employees and guests in the past.

A woman in Victorian clothing has been seen in the upstairs hotel rooms, and guests of the hotel have reported voices arguing in the rooms only to find out that no guests were checked into that room for the night.

In the downstairs shops, apparitions of both a man and woman from different time periods have been seen and the feeling of being watched is constant, state the employees.

CEMETERY

The cemetery at Leavenworth was the main burial ground for railroad workers in the area. Local residents in the area have reported seeing lanterns floating through the cemetery grounds and hearing whistling. The sounds of hammering metal, perhaps hammering spikes from building the railroad, bellow from the cemetery on certain nights.

Directions from Leavenworth to The Ivy Wild Inn: Head Northeast on US-2, slight right at North Miller Street, continue on North Miller Street.

THE IVY WILD INN

410 N Miller Street, Wenatchee, WA 98801
(509) 293-5517 △ (866) 783-4754 △ www.theivywildinn.com

The Ivy Wild Inn Bed and Breakfast offers four bedrooms in the historic home. Legends state that a former owner lived in the house with his wife, and while he was out traveling for business, she would invite her lover over for a tryst.

On one of these occasions, her husband came home early to surprise his wife and found her in bed with her lover. Enraged, he killed the man. To this day you can hear the husband walk up the stairs to the bedroom over and over, repeating the fateful scene that changed his life forever.

Directions from the Ivy Wild Inn to East Wenatchee Cemetery: Head north on North Miller Street toward 5th Street, turn right at 5th Street, turn right at North Wenachee Avenue, slight right to merge onto Stevens Street, take ramp to North Valley Mall Parkway, turn left at North Valley Mall Parkway, turn right at 9th Street NE, turn left at North Eastmont Avenue, turn right at 10th Street NE.

EAST WENATCHEE CEMETERY

1301 10th Street NE, East Wenatchee, WA 98802

In the evening, reports coming from the cemetery grounds are abundant of the dead rising and wandering around. One solider even comes back and wanders the tombstones in his full uniform. On the west side of the cemetery, a dark shadowy man has been seen walking near the orchard and darting through the fruit trees.

SIGHTINGS: OLD BRICK SCHOOLHOUSE

Waterville, WA 98858

The schoolhouse was built in 1864. Neighbors over the years and passersby say they can hear children playing forgotten games on the grounds as well as hearing a swing set squeak as the swings move. The only problem is that the swing set was removed years ago.

Visitors to the schoolhouse at night claim candles will not stay lit in the old building, and if you use any electronic equipment, such as flashlights, camera, etc., the batteries will run down immediately and will not function properly.

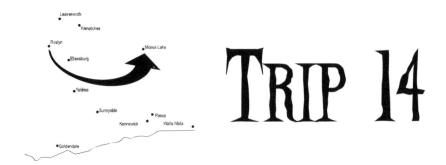

Trip 14

Roslyn to Moses Lake

Beginning Directions: From Interstate 90 exit 80, turn left at Bullfrog Road, slight left at WA 903.

Roslyn

Roslyn, WA 98941

You would be hard pressed to find an original building in Roslyn that wasn't inhabited by at least one unworldly spirit.

The Brick Tavern

The Brick Tavern is the most famous haunted location in Roslyn. The two spirits are a miner that hangs around the bar area and a little girl that may have lived in the apartment upstairs. Items are moved and the sounds of daily life in the late 1800s are common in this historic bar, including piano music and chopping wood.

The Theater

The Theater used to be the town morgue—who knows how many spirits still hang around to watch the latest movie?

Visit the Brick Tavern where coal miner spirits still relax.

PIONEER RESTAURANT AND SODY-LICIOUS BAR

A logger and two women, one of which you can see looking out of the upstairs window, haunt the Pioneer Restaurant and Sody-Licious Bar next door to The Brick Tavern.

SCHOOL HOUSE

The old school house has been known for its ghosts as well. Patrons report that books move, chairs rearrange themselves, and lights turn on and off.

MINE SHAFTS AND CEMETERY

Residents have heard yelling emanating from the old mine shafts and, of course, the cemetery is haunted.

Roslyn got its start as a coal-mining town in 1886. On May 10, 1892, forty-five miners died in Mine Number 4. If you weren't killed from the explosion, you would have asphyxiated within minutes. Twenty-nine widows and ninety-one orphans were left to pick up the pieces; some families filed suit against the Pacific Coal Company only to be compensated with a thousand dollars each.

The town is built directly over a shaft to Mine Number 4, and when the explosion hit, the whole town shook, with oil-soaked timbers shooting out of the shaft igniting more than twenty roofs.

The cemetery in Roslyn is a total of twenty-five separate cemeteries situated next to each other on fifteen acres of land. Some houses in Roslyn have cemeteries of their own on the property. More than 5,000 men, women, and children of mainly immigrants are buried in Roslyn, many of whom had a tragic, untimely death.

Made famous by the 1990 television show *Northern Exposure*, Roslyn still hangs on even after the last mine closed in 1962. Currently, the high-end resort of Suncadia is promising to keep the town alive by proximity.

Directions from Roslyn to Thorp Cemetery: I-90 E exit 101 for Thorp Highway, turn right at South Thorp Highway, sharp right at Thorp Cemetery Road.

THORP CEMETERY

Thorp Cemetery Road, Thorp, WA 98946

An Indian woman who was wrongfully lynched by an angry mob in the late 1800s has been seen in the cemetery wandering around. Other sightings of her have been on a grand, ghostly white horse slowly gliding past the graves.

The cemetery is on private property.

Directions from Thorp Cemetery to Liberty Theatre: I-90 E take exit 109 for Canyon Road toward Ellensburg, turn right at South Canyon Road, slight right at Main Street, turn right at West 5th Avenue.

LIBERTY THEATRE

111 E Fifth Street, Ellensburg, WA 98926
(509) 925-9511 △ www.hallett.com

Patrons and employees to the theatre have experienced the bathroom doors opening and closing on their own, and after the theater is closed up for the night, screams are heard bellowing from the building.

Directions from the Liberty Theatre to Kamola Hall: East on East 5th Avenue, turn left at North Pine Street, turn right East 8th Avenue/East University Way.

KAMOLA HALL AT CENTRAL WASHINGTON UNIVERSITY

400 East University Way, Ellensburg, WA 98926

During the 1940s, a young girl received news that her fiancé had been killed in the war. She was so distraught that she hung herself from the attic rafters in Kamola Hall near her dorm while she attended school in Ellensburg.

On the top floor of the hall, where her room was located, students report doors and closets opening and closing, locking and unlocking by themselves, and some students have even felt warm breath on their shoulder as they try and study.

SIGHTINGS: HELL'S HOLE

Madistash Ridge near Ellensburg, WA

In 1997, on Art Bell's Dreamland radio show, Mel Waters tells a story of a "bottomless shaft" near Ellensburg in the Madistash Ridge. The hole is claimed to be about ten feet wide and is of mysterious origin. Other whispers about the hole claim that men in black appeared one day. Locals and the discoverer of the hole quickly could not remember anything about a hole.

Directions from Kamola Hall to Olmstead Place: Head East on East 8th Avenue, continue on Euclid Way, slight right at East 10th Avenue, continue on East Vantage Highway, turn right at North Ferguson Road, turn left at Kittitas Highway.

OLMSTEAD PLACE STATE PARK

Ellensburg, WA 98926
www.parks.wa.gov

The first homestead in Kittitas County was Olmstead Place and now features a living history farm. At one time, the homestead was used as an Indian fort and visitors to the park report the feeling of being followed around and watched. Some visitors have even seen ghostly Indians near the creek area going about their daily business. A few campers who have stayed the night nearby at the campground have reported hearing a woman screaming and a baby crying at night.

Directions from Olmstead Place State Park to Moses Lake High School: From Olmstead State Park, head east on Kittitas Highway, continue on 4th Avenue, turn right on Main Street, slight left at Railroad Avenue, slight right at Main Street, merge onto I-90 E, exit 179 for WA-17, merge onto South Frontage Road E, turn left at WA-17, continue on South Pioneer Way, turn left at Sharon Avenue E.

Moses Lake High School

803 East Sharon Avenue, Moses Lake, WA 98837

The theater of Moses Lake High School is where all the activity seems to happen. Students and faculty have reported the heavy main stage curtain swaying, and lights turning on and off with no one in the control booth. Reports of hearing footsteps walking up and down stairs and ghostly foot falls walking on the catwalk have been reported when only the janitor has been in the theater area—and long after school has been locked up for the evening. The costume room feels full of people when only one or two people are there.

Directions from Moses Lake High School to Griffith Cemetery: Head east on Sharon Avenue E, turn right at South Pioneer Way, continue on WA-17, turn right to merge onto I-90 E, exit 221 for WA-261 S towards Ritzville, turn left at WA-261, the cemetery is 8.5 miles north of Ritzville on Marcellus Road. Cemetery is on left.

Griffith Cemetery

Adams County, WA

The homesteaders, the Griffiths, set aside two acres for a small cemetery to serve the new pioneer village of Griffith. William Griffith opened a general store and post office in the hopes of starting a small farming town in 1891, but the town was a bust by 1905.

In the cemetery are buried members of the Griffith, Larmer, and Kramer families, as well as some of the neighbors. Mainly children are buried here due to the increased chance of death in the nineteenth century.

When the fog rolls in at night, the children of these families are seen wandering and playing games in the cemetery grounds. Rumors persist that small handprints appear in the dirt on your vehicle when you visit.

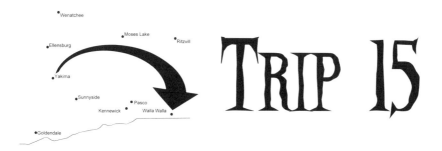

Trip 15

Yakima to Walla Walla

Beginning Directions: From Interstate 90 exit Canyon Road, head South, road will turn into State Highway 821.

Yakima Canyon

Interstate 82, Between Ellensburg and Yakima, WA 98908

The scenic drive takes you off the interstate for a bit as you drive along the river and fierce cliffs. Over the years, many fishermen and farmers to this area report seeing an elderly and a Hispanic man. Stories state that a Hispanic man was an unsolved murder victim, while the elderly man committed suicide in the area.

Directions from Highway 821 to Cherry Park: From Highway 821, turn right to merge onto Interstate 82 East toward Yakima, exit 31B for North 1st Street, turn left at north 4th Avenue.

Cherry Park

North 4th Avenue & Cherry Street, Yakima, WA 98902

Ghostly children have been seen and heard playing in Cherry Park. Reports claim ghostly children are heard running around, screaming at the top of their lungs, and there is a strong smell of sulfur coming from the area.

This park is not supposed to be the friendliest park in town; check it out with caution.

Directions from Cherry Park to Capital Theater: Head South on N 4th Avenue toward West C Street, turn left at West Yakima Avenue, turn right at South 3rd Street.

CAPITAL THEATER

19 South Third Street, Yakima, WA 98901
(509) 853-8000 △ www.capitaltheater.org

The Capital Theater was built in 1920 by Frederick Mercy as the largest vaudeville theater in the Pacific Northwest. By the 1970s, the theater had moved from vaudeville to motion pictures and slowly declined until talk of demolition was eminent. A few days after the decision was made to tear down the theater, the citizens of Yakima banded together and saved the building. But a fire broke out that nearly destroyed the historic building just a few days later. Two years after the fire, the theater reopened, fully restored, and now lives on.

The spirits of the theater must approve of the restoration as they still hang around to give patrons and employees a spook now and then. Janitors late at night report hearing voices and seeing spirits walk around the theater.

Directions from Capital Theater to St. Paul's School: North on South 3rd Street, turn left at East Yakima Avenue, turn left at South 12th Avenue, turn right at West Chestnut Avenue.

ST. PAUL'S SCHOOL

1214 W Chestnut Avenue, Yakima, WA 98902
(509) 575-5604

Legend surrounding the St. Paul's School claims that a sister who taught at the school died an untimely death on the fourth floor of the structure. Reports are, you can hear screams and noises all over the school. In the restroom, the sounds of the water turning on and off and toilets flushing can be heard, even though no faucets have been turned on or toilets flushed.

Directions from St. Paul's School to Yakima Valley Memorial Hospital: West on West Chestnut Avenue, turn left at South 28th Avenue, turn right at West Tieton Drive.

Yakima Valley Memorial Hospital

2811 Tieton Drive, Yakima, WA 98902
(509) 575-8000

The Yakima Valley Memorial Hospital, like many you may enter, has its own group of spirits hanging around. Perhaps they are still fighting for their lives or just didn't want to pass on.

The morgue area is a hotspot of activity. The elevator seems to carry ghostly passengers, with reports of cold drafts in the elevator. It seems to take on a mind of its own, stopping at floors you did not press and letting on and off ghostly passengers as you try and make it to your floor.

Many of the hospital staff have seen people out of the corner of their eyes either walking or sitting; when they turn to get a better look, they find themselves alone.

Sightings: Aliens

Yakama Indian Reservation, WA

Ghost lights seen above the Yakama Indian Reservation. Hundreds have reported seeing strange lights above the reservation and many report a strong feeling they should not have been witness to this event.

Some say that, under the Yakama Indian Reservation, an alien base is located.

Directions from Yakima Valley Memorial Hospital to Fort Simcoe State Park: East on W Tieton Drive, turn right at S 26th Avenue, turn left at W Nob Hill Blvd, take ramp onto I-82 E, exit 37 for US-97, turn right at Fort Road, turn left at Fort Road, turn left at Mill Creek Canyon Road, turn right at Fort Simcoe Road, turn left at Fort Simcoe State Park.

FORT SIMCOE STATE PARK

**Seven miles west of White Swan
Interpretive Center open from April 1 through October 1
9:30am - 4:30pm**

Visitors and fort employees have claimed to have seen a ghostly woman looking out of one of the windows in the commander's house. She is said to be the young bride of one of the commanders who fell ill and ended up dying of fever in the 1800s.

The park is also thought to be the origination of the famous Toppenish Green Lights in 1973.

Located seven miles west of White Swan, the park is 200 acres on the Yakama Indian Reservation. The fort was originally a 1850s military installation, established as a peacekeeper between the Indians and settlers.

Directions from Fort Simcoe State Park to Whitstran: Return to I-82 E, take exit 80 for Gap Road, turn left a North Gap Road, turn right at West Johnson Road, slight right at West Old Inland Empire Highway.

WHITSTRAN

West Old Inland Empire Highway, Whitstran, WA 99350

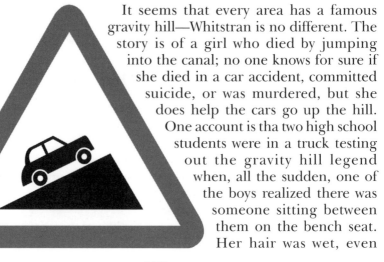

It seems that every area has a famous gravity hill—Whitstran is no different. The story is of a girl who died by jumping into the canal; no one knows for sure if she died in a car accident, committed suicide, or was murdered, but she does help the cars go up the hill. One account is tha two high school students were in a truck testing out the gravity hill legend when, all the sudden, one of the boys realized there was someone sitting between them on the bench seat. Her hair was wet, even though no water was in the canal at the time, and she disappeared as quickly as she came.

Of course, what you do is turn off your car, put it in neutral, and the car will roll up hill. Some even say if you put powder or dirt on the bumper, you will see fingerprints of the ghostly hands pushing your car. A few eyewitnesses stated seeing a girl with wet hair pushing their car up the hill and others have claimed of seeing a girl jumping into the canal.

Directions from Whitstran to Pioneer Park: From Old Inland Empire Highway, turn right at Horne Drive, continue on North Webber Canyon Road NE, turn left to merge onto I-82 E, take exit 102 to merge onto I-182 E, continue on US-12, continue on WA-12, turn right at East Rees Avenue, turn right at North Park Street, turn left at Alder Street.

PIONEER PARK

Alder & Division - Walla Walla, WA 99362

Rumors of a beautiful woman hitchhiker have surrounded Pioneer Park for centuries. Complete with an aviary, Pioneer Park offers forty-seven historic acres. Started in 1901, it is home to a 1909 bandstand, rose garden, an iron fountain dating from 1910, playgrounds, trails, and of course, an aviary that holds more than sixty different species of birds.

Locals have seen a beautiful glowing woman standing by the side of the road at the edge of the park, she disappears when you try to approach her. Is she responsible for the blue mist that hovers in the trees at the century old park?

 # SIGHTINGS: THE HAUNTED TUNNEL

Waitsburg, WA 99361

Be careful; motorists have seen a headless man walking in the tunnel. He is the victim of his machinery, when it overtook and decapitated him while building the tunnel for the road. Some claim to have seen him wandering headless with his machinery following behind.

Trip 16

Carson and Goldendale

Beginning Directions: From State Road 14 exit Hot Springs Avenue, head North.

Carson Hot Springs

372 St. Martin's Road, Carson, WA 98610
(509) 427-8292 △ (800) 607-3678 △ www.carsonhotspringresort.com

In 1876, Lsadore St. Martin stumbled across the hot springs while on a hunting expedition. St. Martin brought his wife to the springs to heal her neuralgia, a painful disorder of the nerves. Soon after the couple arrived, word spread about the healing waters and people came from all over for relief from the mineral hot springs.

In 1901, St. Martin built the hotel and later added the cabins and bathhouse in 1923. In the historic hotel, visitors have reported feeling a cold breeze sweep past them when upstairs, even when no windows and doors are open. Reports of a shadowy figure and electrical malfunctions are persistent in one of the upstairs bedrooms as well. Some say it is the former owner still hanging around keeping an eye on his hot springs.

Directions from Carson Hot Springs to Maryhill Museum: From the Hot springs, only one hour further is the Maryhill Museum, turn left at State Road WA-14, and turn right at Maryhill Museum Drive.

MARYHILL MUSEUM

35 Maryhill Museum Drive, Goldendale, WA 98620
(509) 773-3733 △ www.maryhillmuseum.org
Open 7 days a week 9am - 5pm, March 15 through November 15

Built by Samuel Hill, a successful entrepreneur in 1914, Maryhill Museum started as an idea of hoping to create a Quaker settlement on 6,000 acres along the Columbia River. First, he built a small town including a church, general store, and post office. Unsuccessful due to the remote locale, he stopped building onto his mansion in 1917.

One of his close friends convinced him to turn his mansion into an art museum, and after acquiring many pieces of art, he was privileged to have the museum dedicated by Queen Marie of Romania in 1926.

Only a few years later, Hill died, leaving his museum still unfinished. In 1940, the museum was finally unpacked and ready for the public—and has been open ever since.

Many past docents, curators, and even cleaning crews have reported hearing unexplained sounds and other strange noises in the mansion. Some unexpecting visitors have reported feeling cold spots in different parts of the museum. Is this Hill still working on his museum or his dream of a Quaker settlement?

TRIP 17

SPOKANE

Beginning Directions: From Interstate 90 exit South Craig Road, head North, turn left at West Thorpe Road.

FAIRCHILD AIR FORCE BASE

6 West Castle Street, Spokane, WA 99011

Fairchild Air Force Base had several unfortunate deaths in 1994. On June 24, four airmen were killed as a result of one of the last B-52s left at the airbase stalling and clipping a set of power lines during a practice flight for an upcoming air show. The aircraft plummeted to the ground at a staggering rate of 170 mph, exploding upon impact in a huge fireball and spreading debris a total of five miles in all directions.

Just a few days earlier, on June 20, an ex-service member, Dean Mellberg, entered the base hospital and started shooting, killing five people and wounding twenty-three others. Only a year prior the gunman was at Fitsimmons Army Medical Center for psychiatric treatment and was discharged for unruly conduct. Records state he was caught by a dorm chief having sexual relations with his mother. A security officer nearby shot Mellberg during his killing spree.

Besides the numerous Air Force personnel who claim to have unexplained events happen to them around the nuclear storage area where the B-52 plane crashed during practice, and the strange sounds at the hospital where the insane shooter killed and wounded many people, there is a Hanger where a KC-135 aircraft is kept that has its own disturbances. Fuel leaks to the plane come and go for no reason, as well as power loss to the hanger and secured objects that fall and move on their own.

SIGHTINGS: GOAT MAN FAIRCHILD AIR FORCE BASE

Security personnel at the Air Force base have reported on many occasions through the years seeing a "Goat Man." One security officer saw the Goat Man by the Nuclear Storage Area running at his vehicle at about 1:30am. After reporting this incident to his team leader, other security officers admitted to seeing the same thing while on patrol at night.

Another sighting was again at the Nuclear Storage Area; an officer noticed the motion sensor security camera click on and saw the Goat Man scale the fence and disappear out of sight.

Many more sightings of this creature have been reported, mainly in the same area of the Air Force Base.

Directions from Fairchild Air Force Base to Patsy Clark Mansion: Head Northeast on West Castle Street, turn left at Chennault Avenue, turn right at Fairchild Highway, turn left at North Vet Road, turn left at North Pol Road, continue on Fairchild AFB, turn right at South Christensen Road, turn right at WA-2, take I-90 E to Spokane, exit 280 for Maple Street, merge onto West 5th Avenue, turn left at South Walnut Street, turn left at West 2nd Avenue.

PATSY CLARK MANSION

2208 West 2nd Avenue, Spokane, WA 99204

Patsy Clark, a mining tycoon, built the 12,000-square-foot mansion in 1897. Clark collected items from all over the world to furnish his grand home. He died in 1915, and his wife stayed on in the beloved mansion until she passed away in 1926.

After many reincarnations, the home is finally being restored, as close as possible, to its original grandeur and will be reopened as a law

Three ghosts are said to still inhabit the Patsy Clark Mansion.

office. Tours are to be offered of the mansion, but no information is available at this time.

Reports of the ghosts usually surface from incidents in the wine cellar. When the mansion was a restaurant, employees reported that wine bottles would fly across the room and sometimes be rearranged. Rumors are that three ghosts hang around the property.

I wonder if the renovations are going to either increase the activity or perhaps put the spirits to rest, finally satisfied that the house is back to its original state.

Directions from Patsy Clark Mansion to Campbell House: East on West 2nd Avenue, turn left at South Hemlock Street, turn left at West 1st Avenue.

CAMPBELL HOUSE

2316 West 1st Avenue, Spokane, WA 99201
www.northwestmuseum.org

The Campbell house was built in 1898 for the railroad and mining tycoon, Amasa B. Campbell, and his family. Amasa died in

Visitors to the Campbell House have seen the spirit of a little girl in an upstairs bedroom.

1912, but his wife, Grace and daughter, Helen, continued to live at the residence until Grace's death in 1924. Helen then gave the home to the Eastern Washington State Historical Society and the Cheney Cowles Museum.

The house has since been restored with the Cheney Cowles Museum on the first floor of the home. In this home, you may hear children running and playing and sometimes a child's laughter out of nowhere. Some visitors claim of seeing a little girl in one of the upstairs bedrooms. One visitor to the house felt a hand on his back, and took a photograph, which revealed a woman's head and shoulders in the nearby room.

Directions from Campbell House to Love and Laughter Daycare: East on West 1st Avenue, turn left at South Cedar Street, turn left at West Sprague Street, slight left at West Riverside Avenue, take ramp onto North Maple Street, slight right at North Maple Street.

LOVE AND LAUGHTER DAYCARE

4125 N Maple Street, Spokane, WA 99205
(509) 326-6602

Children at this daycare have often reported seeing unknown children they don't know standing just outside of the group. On one occasion, a worker at the daycare claimed to have been changing two toddlers' diapers in the bathroom when she had to leave suddenly. Upon returning to finish up with the two toddlers, an unseen force shut the door to the bathroom. After pushing hard for at least a minute, she still could not open the door. Finally, the door opened on its own as if it had never been shut tight.

Other workers at the daycare have claimed to chase a young boy into a bathroom only to discover they are chasing a ghost when no one is found. Other reports from the daycare claim to have seen ghostly children outside playing ring-around-a-rosy and other games.

Directions from Love and Laughter Daycare to Center State and Ella's Supper Club: North on North Maple Street, turn left at West Rockwell Avenue, turn left at North Ash Street, slight left at North Maple Street, exit West 1st Avenue.

CENTER STAGE & ELLA'S SUPPER CLUB
1017 W 1st Avenue, Spokane, WA 99201
www.spokanecenterstage.com

This building was used for many years as a Masonic Hall. The members of the secret society do not like the modern day patrons and businesses snooping around their beloved building. The basement is a hub of activity for the long-ago Masonic members; items move by themselves and whispers are heard coming from dark corners.

Center Stage and Ella's Supper Club. Whispers have been heard in the basement of the former Masonic Hall.

The building has housed several businesses, and the latest is Center Stage on the second floor and Ella's Supper Club on the third floor, leaving the basement for ballroom dances and classes. Unfortunately, Center Stage and Ella's Supper Club, too, has recently announced its closure. What is the next business that will brave the Masons who haunt this local?

Directions from Center Stage & Ella's Supper Club to The Met: East on West 1st Avenue toward South Monroe Street, turn left at South Lincoln Street, turn left at Sprague Avenue.

THE MET

901 W Sprague Avenue, Spokane, WA 99204
www.mettheater.com

In 1915, the Metropolitan Performing Arts Center, then called the Old Clemmer Theater, brought the first silent movies to Spokane. The theater no longer shows movies, but is a beautifully restored theater featuring music, auctions, and other performances.

Investigators have reported four different ghosts that reside at the Met. A previous caretaker of the performance hall still keeps watch on the building; he is called "Gary." A young woman who continues to look for her children has also been seen and heard at the theater. A young boy plays pranks on the living and, lastly, an older maintenance man who was once employed by the theater, has been heard working on different forgotten projects around the theater. Many reports of hearing different sounds and even names being called out are common.

Directions from the Met to Deaconess Hospital: West on Sprague Street, turn left at South Monroe Street, turn left at West 5th Avenue.

DEACONESS HOSPITAL

800 West 5th Avenue, Spokane, WA 99204

The Deaconess Hospital has a spirit that hangs around the north elevator. Legend states that Charlie, a hospital maintenance worker, was working on the elevator and was crushed when the elevator malfunctioned. Apparently, Charlie will take the elevator to the floor he thinks you should go to. The button lights will show the correct floor you pushed, but when the doors open, you will find it is the wrong floor.

Hospital personnel have reported seeing unexplained shadows moving about the hospital. Is this Charlie or maybe some of the unfortunate who passed in the hospital?

Directions from Deaconess Hospital to Davenport Hotel and Tower: East on West 5th Avenue, turn left at South Wall Street, turn left at West Sprague Avenue, turn left at South Post Street.

DAVENPORT HOTEL AND TOWER

10 South Post Street, Spokane, WA 99201
(509) 455-8888 △ (800) 899-1482 △ www.thedavenporthotel.com

Opening in 1914, the Davenport Hotel was the finest hotel in the West, equipped with air conditioning, central vacuum, the largest private telephone branch exchange, and the most complicated plumbing system

Does Mr. Davenport still watch over the Davenport Hotel?

at that time. The Davenport was the idea of Spokane's local barons who wanted a fine establishment where prospective investors could be wined and dined in a fine style. The men approached Louis Davenport to run the hotel after building two wildly successful local businesses. Davenport took up the challenge and was known for his perfection, including having housekeeping press paper money and wash coins so change would be pristine when given to customers.

The hotel attracted every celebrity of its time, including many presidents in the twentieth century. In 1945, the hotel was sold and Davenport passed away in his suite at the hotel, in 1951, after seeing its decline. By 1987, when the last Davenport descendant died, plans of demolishing the hotel went into place. But due to the asbestos in the building, the plans were scratched.

The year 2000 was a new beginning for the historic hotel. After two years, the new owners opened the restored and expanded grand hotel. During the restoration, workers had many unexplained events happen to them. One crew complained of strange sounds coming from a bathroom on the fourth floor. Vanity doors sounded like they were being opened and slammed shut and banging around from the housekeeping crew as they were rushing to quickly get done. Upon investigation, no one was in the bathroom let alone cleaning.

Other workers had seen a woman in white floating through the hallways on the fourth floor. The electrical crews working on the elevators were left scratching their heads on many occasions as reports of the service elevator stopping on several floors before finally reaching the floor that was called. No one else was working in the hotel except for the crew that called the elevator. The main elevators had their own set of problems; they were known to go to different floors on their own all night long as if ghostly guests were still going about their business.

Is all this activity due to the restoration that took place? The hotel was coming back to life and I'm sure that Mr. Davenport would have been proud, as his ghost must have been watching.

SIGHTINGS: DEVIL LIGHTS

Outside Spokane, WA

Seen just outside of Spokane, the devil lights resemble several red eyes. One of the stories is that the lights are attributed to a cult mass suicide and are supposed to be the restless spirits of those who died.

Another theory is that they are the spirits from a group of college kids who disappeared in the early 2000s. The students were eco-terrorists and apparently known for sabotaging logging equipment. After they disappeared, the lights appeared, and if you try to investigate, you cannot find them—they are always just out of reach.

Directions from Davenport Hotel and Tower to Double Tree Hotel: North on N Wall Street, turn left at Riverfront Park, turn left at W Main Avenue, turn left at N Division Street, turn left at W Spokane Falls Blvd., turn right at Spokane Falls Court.

DOUBLE TREE HOTEL

322 N Spokane Falls Court, Spokane, WA 99201
(509) 455-9600 △ (800) 484-9600 △ www.doubletree.com

During a Halloween party in 1998 held on the fifteenth floor Gold Room of the Double Tree, an unfortunate man committed suicide. Since then guests have reported shadowy forms and strange noises, mainly on the fifteenth floor, but reports have surfaced from all over the hotel.

Directions from Double Tree Hotel to Monaghan Hall: South on North Spokane Falls Court, turn right at West Spokane Falls Boulevard, turn left at Bernard Street, turn left at West Main Avenue, turn left at North Division Street, turn right at East Sharp Avenue, turn right at North Addison Street, turn left at East Boone Avenue.

MONAGHAN HALL

502 East Boone Avenue, Spokane, WA 99258

Built in 1898 by the self-made Irishman James Monaghan, the three-story house with a turret reflects the success of Monaghan. Born in Ireland in 1833, Monaghan was orphaned by the age of three. Raised by his grandparents, he followed his older brother to New York when he was seventeen years old and started to make his mark on this new country. Making his way to the northwest, he finally settled in Colville, just north of Spokane, ending up owning ferries, helping with the organization of the Northern Railroad, and other ventures that continued throughout his lifetime.

Ghostly footsteps follow students in Monaghan Hall.

While Monaghan had great success, including a visit from President Theodore Roosevelt at his Spokane residence in 1903, he also had many tragic events. In 1895, his wife passed away, leaving him with four children under the age of ten. His son died in the line of duty in 1899 by natives while in Samoa. Monaghan also got hit hard when the panic of 1893 took hold of the nation.

But through it all, he was named one of Spokane's millionaires in 1909 and continued to invest in railroads and gold mines until his death in 1916, at the age of seventy-five. The funeral procession for James Monaghan was one of the largest in Spokane's history, including up to 100 cars that led to Fairmount Cemetery.

Monaghan's beloved home was sold to Gonzaga University in 1942, and became home of the Music Conservatory. Gonzaga University is currently a private school founded by Jesuits. The students and some of the Fathers have had many different experiences in the home. Organ music is heard often; some say the song that bellows from the instrument is the one played at James Monaghan's funeral. One housekeeper even saw the organ keys moving by themselves. One of the Fathers heard a flute playing outside his office door; upon investigation, no one was there and he later found out the song was the same one heard coming from the organ.

143

A growling noise from the basement storage closet is sometimes reported. Students are frightened of the footsteps that follow them around while in the building and strange fleeting shadows are seen.

In 1975, an exorcism was held; some say the hauntings still go on while others state that all activity has ceased.

Directions from Monaghan Hall to Wilbur-Hahn House: North on North Addison Street, turn right at East Sharp Avenue, turn right at North Dakota Street, Dakota Street becomes East Desmet Avenue, turn right at North Cincinnati Street, turn left at East Trent Avenue, turn right at North Hamilton Street, take I-90 E, exit 283A toward Altamont Street, merge onto East 3rd Avenue, turn right at South Altamont Street, sharp left at East North Altamont Boulevard, turn left at South Mount Vernon Street, turn right at East 19th Avenue.

WILBUR-HAHN HOUSE

2525 E 19th Avenue Spokane, WA 99223

The Wilbur-Hahn House story is right out of a Hollywood movie with murders, wild parties, suicides, and secret rooms. The house was built in 1916 by the prominent couple Ralston Wilber and Sarah Smith. In 1924, the flamboyant Rudolph Hahn bought the house. Hahn was a painter and barber, but advertised himself as a doctor. He used the basement of the house to perform illegal abortions on the wealthy women of the area.

Hahn was famous for his parties and once hosted Lieutenant J. Doolittle, famous for the Doolittle Raid. He had a tempestuous relationship with his wife, which resulted in many loud fights that bellowed from the mansion, and they even had been divorced only to remarry. During one of these fights she shot herself in the head, but only after missing several times, and when she finally got it right, she missed her brain and bled to death—or did Hahn shoot her? No one will ever know.

A few years after his wife's tragic death, Hahn accidentally killed a woman while performing an abortion and was convicted of manslaughter. After a $1000 fine and probation, he moved into the New Madison Apartments. On August 6th, 1946, six years after his wife died, he was found dead in his apartment with a bayonet in his chest. A small-time hood named Delbert Visger was arrested for his murder and claimed it was a robbery gone wrong.

Rudolph Hahn was quite the character. He once got so drunk he drove his car into his pool; another time, Spokane residents found him walking down the road with his best suit and slippers on. Some say he hid his abortion money in the house and forgot where he put it.

After the house sat empty for nearly twenty years, it was bought and a string of residents seem to move in and out rather quickly. Residents now report shadowy figures and lights turning on and off as well as doors that lock and unlock and open and close by themselves. Shouting and screaming can be heard from the street when the house is vacant, and residents have claimed of waking up and hearing a late-night party downstairs with 1920s music and all.

The house is currently a private residence. Please do not disturb.

Directions from Wilur-Hahn House to Minnehaha Park: East on East 19th Avenue, turn left at South Ray Street, turn right at East 17th Avenue, turn left at South Freya Street, continue on North Greene Street, turn right at East Grace Avenue, turn left at North Freya Street, turn right at East Euclid Avenue.

MINNEHAHA PARK

4055 E Euclid Avenue, Spokane, WA 99207

Minnehaha Park is one of Spokane's most popular rock climbing parks featuring an assortment of easy to more challenging short routes on granite cliffs. Climbing has been popular in this park since the 1950s, but that's not what the haunting is from.

Climbers and neighborhood residents out for a stroll have reported children's laughter and the patter of small children running by them in the park late at night.

Directions from Minnehaha Park to Centennial Middle School: West on East Euclid Avenue, turn left at North Freya Street, turn right at East Grace Avenue, turn left at North Greene Street, slight left at North Freya Way, turn left at East Trent Avenue, turn right at North Park Road, turn left at East Broadway Avenue, turn left at North Ella Road.

CENTENNIAL MIDDLE SCHOOL

915 N Ella Road, Spokane, WA 99212

The library of Centennial Middle School is known to have a small old lady with no legs gliding from one area of the library to the next, seemingly looking for something, but not recognizing there are students about. At the side entrance of the library, a man and a woman have been seen hanging from the ceiling. What was this area before it was a school? Why are there so many spirits in this small locale? You will have to investigate to find out.

Directions from Centennial Middle School to Mirabeau Park Hotel & Convention Center: South on North Ella Road, turn right at East Broadway Avenue, slight right to merge onto I-90 E, take exit 291B for Sullivan Road, turn right at North Sullivan Road, turn left at East Mission Avenue.

 MIRABEAU PARK HOTEL & CONVENTION CENTER

1100 N Sullivan Road, Spokane Valley, WA 99037
(866) 584-4674 △ www.mirabeauparkhotel.com

This is a three diamond AAA hotel featuring free wireless internet, the award-winning restaurant "Max at Mirabeau," a laundry service, spa and fitness center.

Mirabeau Park Hotel is known to have several spirits that have checked in permanently. Former employees of the hotel claim seeing a woman and her two small children wandering the halls and frightening maids as they do their morning routine of cleaning and making up the rooms.

Rumors claim that a man committed suicide in a room on the first floor; he has been known to play pranks on the hotel staff and they will not enter his room alone. On the third floor, a man has been known to ask for fresh towels when encountered in the hallway, but when the employees ask which room the man is staying in, he disappears.

Conclusion

...And here we are at the end of our ghostly tour of Washington State! I have tried my best to provide an interesting tour for you and one that you will remember with a scare or two! Some of these places have stories that have even more ghostly goings on than I have written, but this guide was intended to lead you to ask questions and experience the supernatural for yourself.

As I have mentioned in the beginning, remember to be respectful of the living and the dead, and if you choose to check out any of these locales for yourself, obey all laws, signs, and do not enter a location without proper permission from the owner.

I hope you have enjoyed Washington's Haunted Hotspots as much as I have bringing it to you. If you have experienced a ghostly encounter or know of a story or hotspot you would like to share, please feel free to e-mail your story with me at LMHauntings@yahoo.com.

Happy hunting in Washington State! Have fun!

GLOSSARY

COMMON GHOST HUNTING TERMS

The following information is provided by author and ghost investigator, Fiona Broome and appears in her book, *Ghosts of Austin, Texas*. For more information, visit http://hollowhill.com/.

There are many words that ghost hunters use in reference to ghosts and haunted places. You're probably familiar with most of these words, but some may be new or have different meanings when they refer to haunted places.

Afterlife
One of several terms used interchangeably to refer to life after death. The word "afterlife" has been used since 1615, and is generic enough to use in almost any setting and culture. Other popular terms include "crossing over," "the Otherworld," and "the other side."

Most ghost hunters avoid specific religious terms such as "heaven" and "the Summerland" when discussing ghosts, hauntings, and an afterlife.

Aliens
Visitors from other planets. We differentiate aliens from visitors that live in parallel worlds, the Otherworld, or what's generally characterized as the afterlife. Some ghost hunters believe in UFOs and aliens; others don't. Generally, ghost hunters don't mix the two studies.

Anomaly
Something that is out of place and unexplained. In paranormal studies, this word refers to any phenomena that we cannot explain. Example: A lens flare in a photo is not an anomaly if you can see the light source that created it. A orb that cannot be explained is an anomaly.

Apparition
Since the early seventeenth century, this word has referred to a ghost that seems to have material substance. If it appears in any physical form, including a vapor-like image, it may be called an apparition.

Banshee
From the Irish, bean sidhe, meaning female spirit. Most families with Irish ancestors have at least one banshee story if you do enough research, but many people are reluctant to discuss this subject. Her wail does not always mean death. She does not cause anyone to die. She's generally not a ghost.

Clearing, or Space Clearing
This is a process of ridding an area of lingering unpleasant energy. It does not "kill" a ghost. Space clearing may encourage ghosts to cross over, or at least leave the haunted location.

Immediately after a space clearing, ghosts can be noisier or more hostile than usual. An effective space clearing may take three to five days to work. In the most haunted settings, it's usually necessary to repeat the space clearing several times.

Demons
Historically, this term has included deceased individuals. However, since the early eighteenth century, the word "demon" usually refers to an evil spirit, sometimes more powerful than man, but less than Deity. Today, we generally do not use this term to indicate a deceased human being. The female demon, very rarely mentioned, is a demoness.

Demons and possessions are treated like UFOs and aliens. That is, most ghost hunters have an opinion about them, but they rarely discuss them in connection with hauntings. The "Amityville Horror" is one noted exception where the story seemed to include both ghosts and possessions.

Ghosts generally do not attempt to take over a living body. In most cases, they believe that they're still alive and—in their minds—each has his or her own body. They're not interested in anyone else's.

Doppelganger
A concept made popular in the early nineteenth century, especially by Shelley and Byron. The doppelganger is the apparition, or double, of a living person.

This may be paranormal phenomenon, but it's not a ghost. It does not forecast anything tragic.

Dowsing rods
These are usually single rods, split rods, or L-shaped wires or twigs. Some people dowse with pendulums, too. They're popularly used to locate water and oil wells, and to measure energy levels of many kinds. For ghost research, we usually use two L-shaped rods.

In ghost hunting, the investigator loosely carries one rod in each hand, and watches the movement of the rods. When the rods cross or splay wide apart, it usually indicates a haunted location.

It's easy to make your own dowsing rods from coat hanger wire. Cut the wire near the top, and again at the opposite end of the lower section. Do this with two different coat hangers to create two dowsing rods.

You can also purchase ready-made dowsing rods. Be certain that they're long enough for ghost research; the 16-inch length is recommended. Look for dowsing tools that glow in the dark. They're especially useful for ghost hunting.

Hold each one loosely in your hands with your arms extended or your elbows bent at a right angle. The rods should be pointed straight ahead of you, and able to swing on their own.

If the rods are drifting, this could be from the normal movement of your body. However, in haunted places, the pull on the rods is strong and cannot be mistaken for a casual, unconscious movement of your hands.

When you step out of the haunted area, the rods return to their original position.

Some researchers successfully use dowsing rods to find unmarked graves. With practice, it's possible to use the rods to detect other information about the body in the grave and the spirit that may haunt the site.

Ectoplasm

Often referred to as "ecto," this is the physical residue of psychic energy. It's the basis for "slime" used in the Ghostbusters movies. Ectoplasm can be seen by the naked eye, and is best viewed in dark settings, since it is translucent and tends to glow. It is very unusual.

Researchers often describe it as a vivid, *X-Files* kind of lime green. It usually fades from sight gradually.

EMF

The initials stand for Electro Magnetic Field, or Electro Magnetic Frequency. In the broadest terms, EMF is a combination of electrical and magnetic fields. You'll find EMF around power sources, fuse boxes, electrical outlets, computer monitors, microwave ovens, etc.

It's smart to study EMF so that you'll recognize the normal sources of elevated EMF readings.

Constant, clearly defined EMF fields usually have a logical explanation.

Unexplained EMF fields may indicate something paranormal. EMF fields can be measured with various tools, including an EMF meter or a hiking compass.

Entity
An entity is any being, including people, animals, and ghosts. It can also refer to aliens, faeries, mystical beasts, and a wide range of paranormal creatures. If you use this term—and many ghost hunters do—be sure that others understand your context.

ESP
ESP is the abbreviation for Extra Sensory Perception. It means the ability to perceive things beyond the usual five senses of smell, hearing, touch, taste, and sight.

Although these perceptions may be interpreted as sounds or sights, experienced ghost hunters can usually tell the difference between normal detection with the five senses, and things detected with the "sixth sense" or psychic abilities.

EVP
Electronic Voice Phenomena, or the recording of unexplained voices, usually in haunted settings. Sometimes the voices are heard during the investigation. More often, the voices are whispers, understood only when a sound recording is processed, filtered, and amplified with a computer.

When people first recorded EVP, they insisted on total silence so normal noises and talking wouldn't be confused with EVP. More recently, people have deliberately included sounds such as normal talking, white noise, and so on. Some researchers believe that ghosts may need ambient noise to create their own sounds and speech.

Most researchers use digital recorders to save EVP. Once the researcher is at home, he or she uses a computer program to filter out everyday noises, such as airplanes and passing cars. The recording may need to be speeded up or slowed down, or a range of sounds magnified above others.

Faeries
Beings that live in the Otherworld or Underworld, parallel to our world and not far from it. Many researchers who readily accept the reality of ghosts don't believe in faeries. Similar to the subject of aliens and UFOs, it's best to keep faerie research clearly separated from your ghost hunting.

Fear
Most ghost hunters have a healthy respect for ghosts and paranormal phenomena. Many ghost hunters enjoy a "good scare." However, if you feel genuinely alarmed or frightened while ghost hunting, it's prudent to leave that location. It may have been your imagination, but there may be something (or someone) truly dangerous nearby.

Ghost hunting should always be interesting, and sometimes entertaining. If it's not, you may be at risk. Ghost hunting should never become a "dare" or an endurance test.

If you're truly frightened in any setting—haunted or not—leave immediately. If this happens regularly when you're ghost hunting, choose a different hobby.

Ghost

A sentient entity or spirit that visits or lingers in our world, after he or she lived among us as a human being. We've also seen evidence of ghostly animals and pets.

Ghost hunters generally use other terms for other beings such as aliens and faeries.

Ghoul

This word has been mistakenly used to mean a ghost. "Ghoul" comes from Middle Eastern lore, where it may refer to an evil spirit that robs graves.

Haunted

Describes a setting where ghosts, poltergeists, and/or residual energy seem to produce significant paranormal activity. The word "haunt" originally meant to frequent.

Hollow Hill

Hollow Hill is the name of Fiona Broome's ghost hunting website! http://www.HollowHill.com. It is one of the oldest and most trusted ghost-related websites online.

Medium

This word usually refers to something in the middle, relative to size or duration.

In ghost hunting, it means anyone who is able to convey communications from departed spirits. That is, the person is able to maintain a position between the world of the living and those who've crossed over, and talk with (or for) those on the other side.

This term was popularized in the mid nineteenth century and is often used interchangeably with the word "psychic." (Compare that definition in this glossary.)Some people call themselves psychic mediums because they can communicate with the other side, but also sense other paranormal energy and/or work with ESP.

Occult
From the Latin, meaning something that is concealed or covered. Since the sixteenth century, it has meant anything that is mysterious. Today in America, it generally refers to magical, mystical and experimental studies.

Orb
An orb is a round, whitish or pastel-colored translucent area in photos. Generally, these are perfectly circular, not oval. Many researchers believe that they represent spirits or ghosts.

If you're using a digital camera, it's important to differentiate between an area of broken pixels (called an "artifact") and the translucent, circular image that is an orb.

Also, any reflective surface or light source can create a lens flare that looks like an orb. When taking photos, note glass, shiny metal, reflective signs, polished surfaces such as tables and headstones, and lights.

In most cases, ghost hunters do not see orbs when they're at a haunted site. Usually, orbs show up only in photos. They are the most common evidence for hauntings.

Critics often dismiss orbs as lens flares and artifacts. However, unexplained orbs often appear at haunted sites. They're rarely in photos at locations that aren't haunted.

Ouija
From the French and German words for "yes," this is a spelling board used with a planchette. The device is intended to communicate with and through the spirit world, obtaining answers to questions.

Generally, we don't recommend them on serious ghost investigations. Some people are vehemently opposed to Ouija boards. The biggest problem is that researchers can't tell who is really moving the planchette. Even if it is a ghost, the spirit could be playing a prank or lying; the information from Ouija boards is unreliable for ghost research.

Paranormal
The prefix, "para" indicates something that is irregular, faulty, or operating outside the usual boundaries. So, "paranormal" refers to anything outside the realm and experiences that we consider normal.

Parapsychology
The study of mental abilities and effects outside the usual realm of psychology. Parapsychology includes the study of ESP, ghosts, luck, psychokinesis, and other paranormal phenomena.

Pendulum

A small weight at the end of a cord or chain that is usually about six to ten inches long. The movement of the weight, when uninfluenced by other factors, can be used to detect areas of paranormal energy.

Poltergeist

From the German meaning "noisy ghost," this term has been in use since the early nineteenth century to mean a spirit that makes noise, or otherwise plays pranks... usually annoying. Unlike other ghosts, poltergeists can move from one location to another, following the person they've chosen to torment.

Many psychologists believe that poltergeists are not ghosts at all, but some form of psychokinesis or remote activity.

Portal

Literally, a doorway or gate, this term suggests a specific location through which spirits enter and leave our world. When there are multiple phenomena in a confined area, such as an abundance of unexplained orbs, some people call this a "ghost portal."

Possession

When an entity attempts to take control of a body that does not belong to them, it's called a possession.

In ghost hunting, this phenomenon is rare, but some psychics and mediums allow ghosts to speak through them. Sometimes, this can enable the living to communicate directly with the ghost and help him or her to cross over.

In extreme cases, a spirit can maliciously attempt to take over an unwilling person's body. Most ghost hunters will never witness this kind of possession, though it's a popular scene in horror movies. Unwilling possession is often linked to demonic activity.

Proof

There is no "proof" of ghosts when someone is a committed skeptic. People who won't believe in ghosts find other explanations for all scientific evidence of hauntings.

A profound, personal encounter with a ghost or the unexplainable is the only way to change someone's mind about haunted places.

Protection

Some researchers use objects, rituals, routines, tactics, or specific processes to protect themselves against ghostly, demonic, or paranormal intrusions and effects. This is a personal matter and rarely discussed during a ghost hunt.

When you go on a ghost hunt, it's generally smart to carry something that you feel may protect you from evil. Most ghost hunters wear a small cross, Star of David, pentacle, or other religious jewelry. They often conceal it under clothing, or wear it as a ring, earrings, or on a bracelet where it won't be noticed.

Carrying a very big, heavy Bible, an intimidating (and very visible) athame, or a large religious icon is usually considered excessive.

Psi

"Psi" or "psy" is a popular term used to mean any psychic phenomena or psychic abilities. This term is sometimes inclusive of paranormal disturbances as well.

Psychic

From the Greek word meaning *of the soul*, or *of life* (Paul used it in the Bible, I Cor ii, 14), this word usually refers to the world outside the domain of physical law.

"Psychic" can relate to the spirit or the mind, depending upon the context. When someone is described as a psychic, it usually means that he or she is able to perceive things that are outside traditional physical laws and perceptions.

Psychical

A British term used as an adjective or adverb, for what Americans call "psychic."

Psychokinesis or Psycho Kinesis

To move something with the powers of one's mind, alone. It may be a factor in some hauntings, and particularly in poltergeist phenomena. It's usually called "PK." (Also see telekinesis.)

Residual Energy

Many ghost hunters believe that emotionally-charged events leave an imprint or residue on the physical objects nearby.

What distinguishes residual energy from an active haunting is that the energy/impressions repeat consistently, as if on a tape loop. The energy level may increase or decrease, but the content remains the same with each manifestation.

By contrast, in an active haunting, the ghost may respond to environmental stimuli and direct contact.

Sixth Sense

Since normal phenomena are detected with the five senses (smell, taste, touch, hearing, and sight), anything that you experience outside those five senses may be categorized as a sixth sense. Usually, this indicates to psychic detection or ESP.

Since M. Knight Shyamalan's movie of the same name, people usually think that the sixth sense refers primarily to seeing ghosts. In reality, few people see ghosts as full figures or living people.

In ghost hunting, the sixth sense can include everything from the ability to hear ghosts whispering, to an internal visual image from the past, or even a "creepy feeling" that can't be explained.

Sparkles

This paranormal visual effect is sometimes described as the sparkle of embers falling immediately after a fireworks display. These small, sparkling lights usually occur no closer to the camera than ten feet. They are often twenty to fifty feet away, or more. Sparkles are seen during, and especially immediately after, the flash on a camera is used.

Even the most vivid sparkles will not show up on film. They are paranormal phenomena.

"Sparkles" is a proprietary term developed in the 1990s by Fiona Broome during research for Hollow Hill. Other researchers have adopted the term to describe this unique phenomenon.

Spirit

This word comes from the Latin, meaning that which breathes. It means that which animates life, or the soul of the being.

Table Tapping, Table Tipping

A method to communicate with spirits. Usually, several people sit around a table with their hands on it, or holding hands on top of the table. Then, they ask the spirits to reply to communicate by tapping on the table, perhaps once for *yes* and twice for *no*.

Others are successful asking the ghosts to lift the table very slightly to show that they are present. Then, the ghosts may tap their replies, move a Ouija-type platen, or use some other means to communicate with movement around the table.

Tarot

The history of the Tarot deck is still unclear. However, since its use in fourteenth century Italy, "Tarot" refers to playing cards that are also used for fortune-telling or divination.

Telekinesis

From a Greek word meaning any motion that is activated from a distance. Technically, this could describe a remote-controlled toy boat, so most people use the word psychokinesis for ghost research.

Vortex

Since the time of Descartes, this has indicated the rotation of cosmic energy around a central point or axis. Beginning in the mid-nineteenth century, the word "vortex" has meant any whirling movement of energy or particles.

Some people use this term to explain lines or narrow cylinders that appear highlighted in ghost photos.

Ghost Tours

www.seattleghost.com

www.spookedinseattle.com

BIBLIOGRAPHY & WEB RESOURCES

Dwyer, Jeff. *Ghost Hunter's Guide to Seattle and Puget Sound.* Pelican Publishing Company Inc., 2008

MacDonald, Margaret Read. *Ghost Stories from the Pacific Northwest.* August House Publishers Inc., 1995

Smith, Barbara. *Ghost Stories of Washington.* Lone Pine Publishing, 2000

http://www.cityofvancouver.us/

http://maps.google.maps.com/

http://www.georgetownhistory.com/

http://www.historylink.org/

http://www.issaquahhistory.org/

http://www.mcmenamins.com/

http://www.mysterymag.com/

http://news.nationalgeographic.com/

http://www.nps.gov/

http://www.nwsource.com/

http://www.sahs-fncc.org/

http://www.skagitriverjournal.com/

http://seattlepi.nwsource.com/

http://www.seattleghost.com/

http://www.sycamoresquare.com/

http://www.thestranger.com/

http://www.thornewoodcastle.com/

http://www.unexplainable.net/

http://www.wagovmansion.org/

http://www.wikipedia.org/

PLACES INDEX